Tempus Oral History *Series*

voices of Ecclesfield, Grenoside, High Green and Chapeltown

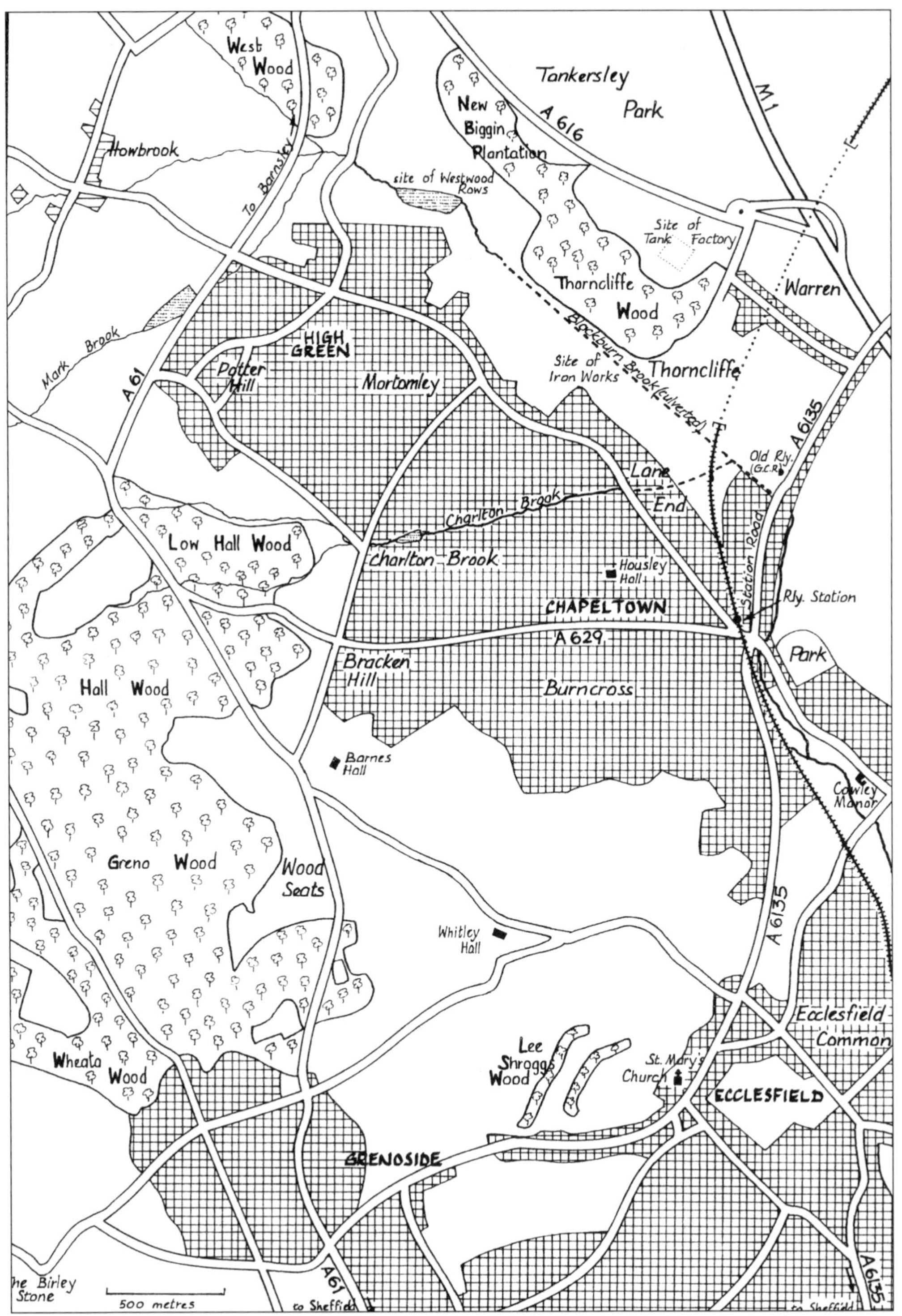

Ecclesfield, Grenoside, High Green and Chapeltown.

Tempus ORAL HISTORY *Series*

voices of
Ecclesfield, Grenoside, High Green and Chapeltown

Compiled by
Joan and Mel Jones
on behalf of
Chapeltown & High Green Archive

First published 2000

Tempus Publishing Limited
The Mill, Brimscombe Port,
Stroud, Gloucestershire, GL5 2QG

ISBN 0 7524 1648 0

Typesetting and origination by
Tempus Publishing Limited
Printed in Great Britain by
Midway Clark Printing, Wiltshire

Cover illustration:
High Green Child Welfare Clinic, Christmas party, c. *1950 in Wortley Road Methodist chapel schoolroom.*

Prefects at Ecclesfield Grammar School, 1950-51, with the headmaster, Mr A.C. Harrison, (centre). The three girls on the headmaster's left, Janet Harrison (next to the headmaster), Aileen Bagshaw and Patricia Walton, have all contributed to this book.

Contents

Introduction 6

Acknowledgements 8

1. Home Life 9
2. Village Life 27
3. Schooldays 43
4. The War Years 55
5. All in a Day's Work 69
6. Leisure and Pleasure 87
7. Special Times 109

Mr Curdew Smith of Townend Road, Ecclesfield, on his 100th birthday in 1952 surrounded by Doreen, Gerald, Betty, Doris and Sandra Wass, Clive Griffiths and June Boulding.

Introduction

As we embark on the twenty-first century we are in danger of taking for granted our current lifestyles and forgetting the unremitting pace of change that was characteristic of the twentieth century. Depending on our age, our great-grandparents, grandparents and even our parents inhabited a world quite different from our own.

At the beginning of the twentieth century motor vehicles were a rarity, and it was still the age of the horse in areas away from railway stations and urban tram networks. On the farm the horse was not totally replaced by the tractor for another fifty years or more. Heavy manual work in iron and steel works, mines and quarries was still the main form of employment for men in the local area and very few married women were employed outside the home. Most children left school at thirteen and many boys went straight into a man's world in foundries and collieries.

At home families were much larger than they are now and housewives and mothers were engaged in an unceasing round of washing, ironing, cooking and cleaning. There was no central heating, no washer dryers, no electric cookers, no electric kettles and toasters, no refrigerators, and no microwaves. Nor were there pre-packed and pre-cooked meals on the shelves of superstores. The local Co-op was the major source of supplies, and sugar, flour and tea were weighed and bagged in the store. Almost all transactions were in cash. Very few people had a cheque book and credit cards and direct debit hadn't been thought of. Telephones were restricted to middle class and professional families. Most people communicated by letter and postcard (there were three deliveries a day).

Leisure time for children was spent as it had been for centuries, playing in woods and fields and on the street in spring and summer, and round the fire reading or listening to stories in the winter. In most families people clustered round a coal fire in winter. The days of a child having his or her own, centrally-heated room with a television set and personal computer were in the far distant future. Church and chapel formed an important part of life with their yearly round of festivals and outings.

But change was inevitable and rapid. In the 1920s radio and talking pictures appeared, cars, lorries, charabancs and buses replaced the horse-drawn wagonette, people were moving into detached and semi-detached houses in the suburbs, council houses with electric lighting and flushing toilets were replacing gas lit cottages with earth closets, and labour saving devices such as vacuum cleaners were being widely advertised. After the Second World War and the gradual disappearance of rationing, the pace of change increased even more markedly and more and more people owned a car, a fridge and a TV set, and foreign holidays became increasingly popular. People were now members of a consumer society where many shopping trips became leisure pursuits rather than grinding chores. These changes were accompanied by earlier retirements and longer life expectancies.

These sharp differences of lifestyle between the present day and the recent past are fully reflected in the recollections gathered together in this volume. They recall and celebrate, people and places, home life and village life, the world of school and the workplace, and leisure time and special events. We have been overwhelmed with the response to our requests for recollections, not only from people living in Ecclesfield, Grenoside, High Green and Chapeltown, but also from people who left the area many years ago to settle in other parts of the country. What has made our task so enjoyable has been the very high quality of the contributions: detailed recollection combined with a fine turn of phrase or a wonderful sense of humour, often accompanied by a selection of photographs not previously published.

The contributions have come in a variety of forms: interviews, submitted tapes, diaries and written pieces. The written pieces have usually followed long interviews and discussions after which contributors have preferred to write everything down – for fear of missing out vital information or, as one person put it, 'to get a tighter weave'. Whatever form recollections have taken, edited versions have normally been returned to contributors for their approval, the exceptions being where deaths have occurred between collecting the original material (as long ago as the late 1970s) and writing up edited versions for this volume.

We are sure that the volume will bring enjoyment and lasting interest to young and old, and long-established residents and relative newcomers alike. We also hope it will inspire readers to record on tape or on paper their own lives. Everyone has a tale to tell!

Joan and Mel Jones
October 1999

Acknowledgements

We would like to thank the following people without whose help this volume would not have been possible:

Harry Allison, Chris Allred, Arthur Andrews, Charles Baines, Marian Barraclough, Ted Bellamy, Alan Boulton, Gwen Boxford, Janet Brewster, Lewis Burrows, Chris and Pete Chapman, Mary Clarke, Clifford Cooper, Marjorie Copley (née Andrews), Marjorie Copley (née Stutchbury), David Crisp, Derek Croft-Smith, Pat Cunningham, John Davis, David Dickinson, Elijah Dransfield, Joe Dunn, Stanley Ellam, Connie Ellis, Anna Evans, Anne Faries, Doris Fox, Ted Frost, Percy Fullwood, Joan Gradwell, Beryl Greaves, John Greaves, Doreen Green,Thelma Gregory, Grenoside Scouts, Janet Haddock, Nellie Hague, Doris Harrison, Janet Harrison, Maisie Hawley, Hugh Hirst, Clara Housley, Kate Hoyland, Jean Huddlestone, Len Hulbert, Lorna Hulley, Elvy Ibbotson, Susan Kelsall, Norman Kirk, Shirley Kirk, Joseph Knott, Carol Limb, Ann Loxley, Wilf Marshall, Ivan Martin, Teresa McSloy, Chris Morley, Alan Morris, Pat Morton, Irene Mulligan, Newton Chambers & Co. Ltd, Eddie Ogle, Margaret O'Toole, Eddie Platts, Roy Portman, Paul Quibell, Derek Renshaw, Harry Ridge, George Robinson, John Rodgers, Mary Salt, Colin Sansam, Len Sansam, Rene and Alan Sharp, Chris Sharpe of 'Old Barnsley' in Barnsley Market, Dave Sheldon, Cyril Slinn, Doreen Smith, Len Smith, *South Yorkshire Times*, Val Sykes, Doris Sylvester, Aileen Thompson, Phil Timmons, Margot Tye, Marjorie Wilson, Doreen Womersley and Herbert Womersley.

The map was drawn by Bob Warburton and the line illustrations are by Eric Leslie. We apologise if we have inadvertently omitted the name of any contributor.

CHAPTER 1
Home Life

'...Camels and elephants were eating the hedges and the ivy off the garden walls...'

Unexpected Circus Visit

I was born in one of the cottages at Wheel Lane Top, Grenoside on 17 January 1900. There were three cottages which stood on the land where the Mormon church now stands. I was the fifth living child of Willis and Mary Ann Andrews (née Cooper). We were crushed for room, having only two bedrooms, a living room and kitchen. My father worked at Silica Brickworks at Oughtibridge.

He got up for work at 4.45 a.m. and one morning could hardly believe his eyes. The garden was full of animals – donkeys, ponies, llamas and others. He got us all up to see, and there was Barnum & Bailey's Circus. All crowded about the crossroads were wagons and caravans of all descriptions; camels and elephants were eating the hedges and the ivy off the garden walls. The circus attendants were struggling to get the animals from the garden which they had cleared of everything – cabbages, potatoes, etc. They got settled eventually but it was too late for father to get to work for 6 a.m. so he had to lose a quarter but the circus master more than compensated him for that and the loss of his vegetables. We were the envy of all the school because we had been so close to the circus and talked about it for days.

Arthur Andrews, born 1900

Home-life at Lane End

I was born on 7 July 1911 in a four-roomed house in a place called Triangle Square! My mother was Nellie Greensmith of Ecclesfield. My father was Sidney Smith, a railway shunter with Newton Chambers. They had five boys (Syd, Tom, Jack, Harry and me) and four girls (Nellie, Kathy, Alice and Phyllis) and one stillborn child. Our house consisted of kitchen, 'house' and two bedrooms. We boys all slept in a double bed, three at the top and two at the bottom. The girls' section was curtained off, and the youngest slept in a cot in mum and dad's room. Often in winter when it was very cold and we had not much bedding I can remember dad coming home from work and throwing his heavy railway jacket over us to keep us warm. On our side of the Triangle lived the Kirkhams, Smiths, Hoylands and Wilkinsons. On the opposite side were the Rowlands, Stevensons and Cooks. In the yard at the end of the houses was a brick building consisting of two earth toilets and a midden for the rubbish and ashes. These were emptied weekly by council workmen, Murgatroyd and Company, who shovelled the contents into wheelbarrows which were tipped in the street. Then a man came with a horse and cart to take everything away. Mum then spread Izal powder around with its very strong smell of disinfectant.

'Triangle Square', Lane End.

Due to the size of our family we were very poor and often very hungry. Mum had to bake bread every other day and she would make oven bottom cakes which were put to cool on the window sill. We had a large earthenware bread pot and the loaves nearly always had no tops, bottoms or sides because we all wanted crusts. These were delicious with lard on. The lard came in pigs' bladders and it was cheap and very good. If the lard was removed carefully from the bladder it could be tied up again and it made a kind of football. To earn a few shillings mum used to go to uncle Jack Massey's butcher's shop in Ecclesfield and scrub the wooden blocks. Uncle Jack would give me a link of polony, which I much appreciated.

On Saturday it was bath night, and we had a zinc bath on the hearth. Hot water came from the boiler next to the fire. Mum would put us in the bath at one end, wash us, and dad would dry us at the other end. We didn't have many clothes and we made use of hand-me-downs! My best Sunday suit went to Mr Worthey's pawnshop on Monday mornings for two shillings ready cash to be redeemed at the weekend.

Len Smith, born 1911

A Shaky Start

I was nearly born in a field! My mother and dad (Joe and Lottie Ashton) were blackberrying on Bromley Lane. My dad was in the field and my mother was on the lane when a man shouted, 'Get out of the way, the bull's loose and is running down the lane!' Mother, in long skirts, as was the fashion, and nine months pregnant, managed to get over the five-barred gate to safety. I was born two weeks later on 25 October 1911.

'Put up an old sheet outside the Sick Room door as a warning barrier. Keep damp with Izal Spray'. From What to do if it's Catching, *issued by Newton Chambers in the early 1930s.*

My first memory is being nursed by my grandma and seeing a white sheet behind her. It wasn't until twenty-five years later that I mentioned it to my mother. She said that I had had scarlet fever and as I was nursed at home they had to have a sheet dipped in disinfectant (probably Izal) hung to the door. I can still remember it today.

Doreen Smith (née Ashton), born 1911

Making Ends Meet

My maternal grandparents, the Galloways, moved from Chapeltown to No. 7 The Common at Ecclesfield (known locally as Enoch Row). My father, Amos Fisher,

Ecclesfield Common, c. 1910.

lodged with them and eventually married my mother, Ursula. They then rented the empty house next door, No. 5. They had twelve children. The eldest, Gertrude, was born in 1892 and the youngest, Mabel, in 1919. Sadly, my father drank heavily, yet I never heard my mother say a wrong word about him or shout back at him. As we children grew older, we would call him to her. She would say, 'Don't let me hear you say such things, remember it's your father you are talking about.' Having said that, he did have his good points too, when he wasn't in drink. He was a good worker. He and four of my brothers worked down Thorpe Hesley Pit. Father worked there for about fifty years and was never late. The miners worked in scandalous conditions – no washing facilities and the work area riddled with rats. When it was 'snap' time they would often find that the rats had eaten it first. After the walk home, no hot bath, just one tap at the sink, with cold water.

To my dying day I shall never know how my mother endured it – all the washing, ironing, baking, cooking and cleaning – and often not knowing where the next meal was coming from. I have seen my mother buy a sheep's head for 9d and make a meal for us all with it, mixed with suet dumplings and plenty of vegetables. There were always two full days of washing, each Monday and Tuesday. Then came the mountains of ironing. Just fancy, ironing white starched collars, she used to make them shine beautifully.

I forgot to mention that my sisters and myself all slept next door at my grandparents' house. My brothers slept at home, it was the only way we could manage. Apart from all the housework, my mother often nursed sick people, leaving the older children in charge at home. Goodness knows how many children she brought into the world, as in those days there were no midwives. She was well known and respected by all the local doctors, in fact, Dr Sands from Chapeltown, offered to pay for her to go to Jessop Hospital in Sheffield to train. Father would not let her go, but still she kept on helping anyone who was ill. I have seen her sit up at night with sick people, and receive 1s 6d for it. I then saw father take it all for drink. If it was possible for her to hide it from him, she would buy material remnants from the Rag Market in Sheffield to make clothes for us. We were all looked after, but she never had anything nice for herself.

Kate Hoyland (née Fisher), born 1910

Westwood Rows, c. 1915

Our living room had a Yorkshire range with an open fire in the centre, an oven on one side and a small boiler for hot water, which held two or three gallons, on the other. Built in one corner was a set pot or copper for heating water and boiling clothes on washday, and providing water for baths. One stone sink with a cold water tap completed the amenities. The set pot served a double purpose as, at the end of washday, we kids were put in it for our weekly bath. On one occasion I complained loudly that the floor was hot, and it was too, as the fire underneath it had not been taken out as was the normal practice before this operation. Baths were also taken in a big oval zinc tub placed in front of the fire.

Outside, across the earth road, each house had a coalhouse and a toilet or, by its more popular name, a closet. This consisted of a wooden seat which led directly into the open midden where all ashes were deposited, the same being emptied, one supposes on contract, by Joe Thorpe, a nearby farmer, with shovel, and horse and cart. He always sat in the cart to eat his midday sandwiches!

After a good many years, Newton Chambers who owned the houses, had water closets fitted. This was a great innovation and the calls of nature increased somewhat till the novelty wore off. The daily paper, *The Sheffield Independent*, was cut or torn into suitable sizes and threaded on a string, and while meditating therein, one read the squares, and in every case the punch line was missing. It was always impossible to find the next square for the continuation of the story. Very frustrating!

Len Sansam

A Yorkshire range.

'Gladys, come and get this burning newspaper off this kid…'

Early Memories

I was born on 16 May 1927 on South Road in High Green. My earliest memory, when I was about three years old, was in my grandfather John Lang's bedroom at the large detached house at Westwood Bottom, where he was ill in bed. He wanted his pipe lighting and, as there was no-one else around, he asked me to light a piece of paper from the bedroom fireplace. I lit a large piece of newspaper but by the time I had passed it to him, it had spread into a large flame. With a look of panic on his moustachioed face, he shouted to my mother, 'Gladys, come and get this burning newspaper off this kid before he bloody well sets me on fire!' That is all I remember of him, as he died not too long after that.

There was another memorable incident in the early hours of the morning of 21 December 1931. The house on South Road only had two bedrooms and myself and our Betty (aged four and seven respectively) had to sleep together in a double bed in the second bedroom. My mother's youngest brother, Harry, who would be a teenager at the time, was staying with us and had to share the bed with our Betty and me. Sharing beds was common then.

It was a dark, cold winter's night and in the early hours we were awakened by a strange sound like a cry of some sort. We asked Uncle Harry what it could be and he told us that it was only a motor car passing, sounding the horn. However, as the sound began again we realised that it was coming from our parents' room and eventually we went to investigate. There was a bright fire burning in the bedroom fireplace and this lit the room with a cosy glow, which enabled us to see that our mother was nursing a brand new baby and this came as a total surprise to us as we didn't have an inkling that we were expecting an addition to the family. In those days children were not told about such matters. The baby was eventually christened Margaret Rose but she has always been known as Peggy. We had a new sister for Christmas.

Eddie Platts, born 1927

Visiting the Dentist

Willie Thorne I heard some grown-ups say, trained in the 1914-18 war to be an Army dentist. As far as I know he did extractions and made false teeth. I hadn't heard about fillings then. There were no appointments in the 1930s. When toothache got unbearable there was nothing for it but to be taken on the bus to Chapeltown, up the steps of Mr

Thorne's surgery and into the usually crowded waiting room, chairs round the outside of the room and an aspidistra on the table in the net-curtained window bay. It was in a brass container and stood on a mingled green and yellow crocheted mat exactly like the one my grandma had on her Singer sewing machine.

Mr Thorne, large, bluff and hearty, fetched his patients himself, calling from the door, 'Who's next?' I felt very small in the big black chair in the middle of the room. The last thing I saw as the gas mask came over my face was the ventilator in the window. It was spinning dizzily round with different lights and colours as I regained consciousness and it was all over. And oh the relief! Everything became wonderfully cheerful, even the cold and the wet as we stood by the Yorkshire Penny Bank opposite the market, waiting for the bus to come down the hill and round the sharp corner. Once, on a Friday winter's evening after a visit to Mr Thorne, mother bought me a diabalo in the market.

Jean Huddlestone (née Kirk), born 1923

Helping Out

Grandma and grandad Baddeley, my mother's parents, lived in the Toll Cottage on Cross Hill, Ecclesfield in the 1930s, opposite the Nurses' Home. They had twelve children, my mother being the eldest. Grandad Baddeley took me to see my first film, *Trader Horn*, at the cinema in the Wicker for helping him on Saturdays. My job was to carry fruit and vegetables from Sheffield Market at 5.30 of an evening when all perishables were sold off cheap. I also helped my grandma by running errands during the week. While I was running errands she collected all the newspapers from the previous week and when I got back she gave me the job of cutting them up. I had to cut 12-inch squares and 6-inch squares and put them in separate piles. She then made a pile about half an inch high of the 12-inch squares and got me to push a nail through and thread a piece of string through about a foot long in which she then tied a knot. These were for the toilet. The 6-inch squares were put two together and a teaspoonful of tea and two teaspoonfuls of sugar were put on each. On the top of the pile of tea and sugar was put a teaspoonful of condensed milk. She then pressed it in a ball and she gave them to me to screw up without squashing the mixture to the paper. These were 'mashings' for her sons to take to work with their 'packing up'.

We also had duties at home. On washday, usually Monday, my sister Jean used to posh the clothes and my sister Enid helped with the ironing although mum always took the iron off the gas stove. My brother, David, and I took it in turns to turn the mangle. My main job was cleaning the fireplace which had the oven combined so all the main cooking was done on it. This had an advantage for me, as in winter, I had the choice of oven plates, which my mother wrapped in blankets and took to bed an hour before going upstairs, to warm the bed.

Lewis Burrows, born 1927

Heat and Light

We moved into our new council house at 117 Greengate Lane, High Green in January 1932. The only source of heating downstairs was the Yorkshire range in the living room. This was a cast-iron structure which housed a coal fire. There was a back boiler behind the fire that gave an abundance of very hot water. There was a shelf over the fire on

Eddie Platts with sisters, Betty and Peggy (front) outside their home on Greengate Lane.

which to stand things, such as plates, to keep warm. In addition there were two warming compartments. In one of these we used to keep sticks for making the fire. It kept them bone dry and easy to burn.

Finally, there was the oven in which mother did all the baking. By turning a draught control lever on the front of the range, the full heat of the fire would be drawn under the oven. Due to her experience and knowledge of the range, my mother could control the temperature of the oven to suit whatever she was baking. Simply by opening the oven door and putting her hand inside to test the temperature, she would know whether or not it was ready for use. Loaves of bread, breadcakes, teacakes and pastries were always baked to perfection and oven-bottom cakes were such that they deserved a gold medal. Only in a coal oven can these be properly baked.

There was no electricity in the house, the illumination being provided by a gas bracket in every room. The jet of burning gas was enclosed in a gas mantle which was made of very flimsy material and could easily be broken when igniting the gas with a lighted match, if it made contact. The best feature of the house was the view from the front window. We could look straight down Greengate Lane and, to the right, there was a good view of farmer Binder's fields.

Eddie Platts, born 1927

Living Next to Granny

War was declared on 3 September 1939 when I was six years old. We lived at 4 Furnace Cottages on Station Road, Chapeltown, next door to my granny. The four old cottages were set at right angles to the road and number four was at the far end. It was very small, one-up, one-down. Close to the house ran a stream, locally called the dyke, and on the other side of it was a wooded slope which is part of Chapeltown Park. Next to the cottages was a small garage workshop. The mechanics used to chat with me during their tea breaks. The war had been expected for some time but I wasn't aware of what was going on, and certainly had no idea of what going to war meant. At six years old I was far more interested in riding my bike, school, my friends and playing with granny's button box.

I don't think mother was too keen on living next door to granny, they had rather an uneasy relationship. I loved visiting her and looking at all her things, especially the photographs on her wall of her seven children. These included my father and his twin brother, George, taken when they were young men. I was always on my best behaviour when I visited her, she was very strict. Her hair was a cap of soft ringlets, of which she was very proud and I think it was a disappointment to her that mine wasn't the same.

Aileen Thompson, born 1933

High Green House

I was born in August 1932 at High Green House, a perfect place for children. It had space and character, a large sprawl of garden and an old orchard, seclusion provided by a

Station Road, Chapeltown, showing the gable end (whitewashed) of Furnace Cottages.

long drive which linked it to the village, a farm attached, fields beyond, as well as the Foster. This was an area of wasteland, mounds left by pit-spoil, good for various games and switch-back riding on bikes, and when I was very young had its resident hermit, Tasker.

Mr Bridge's farm next door provided secret places, play areas for hide and seek, story-telling in the lofts, jumping on and off haystacks – to Mr Bridge's annoyance (although he was very patient), watching the pigs (and rats in the sty walls), daring each other to admire the bull in its stall, having a ride – five of us at a time – on Violet, the carthorse (whom I saw giving birth in the orchard, surprised by size more than anything, as I'd seen kittens arrive). We even dug a large hole in a grassed area by the hen-house and lined it with sacks, made a roof of planks and sods, sat on milk-crates with lit candles while we sang and told stories. We spent long hours, a shifting set of friends, running round the countryside following seasonal pursuits – sledging by the Foster, sliding and skating on Westwood Reservoir, swinging on a rope across the run-off water from the pit-tip, walking to Lady's Folly. Sometimes we tried crossing bogs of pig-muck on planks at Mr Hoggard's piggery, or we ran through the tunnel carrying a stream beneath New Road (someone always fell in), or we swam in Howbrook Reservoir, maybe cycled to picnic by the River Don, near Wortley, and there was always the cinema (9d seats, fish and chips from next-door in the interval) and running errands, helping on the farm or in the garden.

Looking back, I see life as ripples spreading out from High Green House,

High Green House, 'secure and fascinating, a perfect place for children'.

secure and fascinating for a toddler who began to explore the garden, orchard, field (the way to school), farm, village...and later acquired more friends to add to those nearby: Sylvia and George Bridge, Dorothy and Geoffrey Hoggard, Pat Walton. As father was headmaster, I was even taken to Ecclesfield Grammar School for Christmas parties wearing a long dress, red velvet cloak and glory of glories – copper-lustre slippers with pom-poms and elastic crossing the ankles. I still recall seeing a magical world lit by gas-lights as we emerged from the drive. And every year first snows transformed that drive into a hushed, miraculous place. High Green House remains enchanted in my memory.

Janet Harrison, born 1932

Janet Harrison in her element in the grounds of High Green House.

Living in a Prefab

This part of Chapeltown was allotments, and across the road was the Hallamshire Maternity Hospital, and the other houses round about were built in 1932. We've been on Steven Crescent right from the beginning, over fifty years, and they were supposed to be temporary, they gave them a life of ten years. Our first rent was paid in October 1946 – 14s 6d a week. There were sixteen prefabs on this road, and fourteen survive – one as a Tenants' Association office. I'd been demobbed from the Army in July 1946. We were already married and we were on the housing list of the then Wortley Rural District Council while I was in the forces. Almost everyone who moved in here had been in the forces. My wife's father noticed that these prefabs were being put up. They were in three parts and they were erecting one a day on a pre-prepared foundation. The day after a foundation was completed, the erectors moved in and the workmen doing the foundations moved on to prepare the next foundation, and so on down the road.

At first the outside walls were grey – they were made from aluminium – but after about four years they started to paint them about every six years. And they've been re-roofed twice. The first time it was roof strengthening and then about fifteen to twenty years after that they put the present roofing on. When we moved in we had electric lighting, an electric cooker and a fridge – and that was a novelty in those days. But they couldn't do anything else, there was nowhere else to keep your milk cool –

there was no cool cellar. In addition to the aforementioned gadgets there was an electrically-heated wash boiler with a hand operated paddle and fitments to accommodate an Acme rubber roller mangle. Another innovation was that a radio aerial was incorporated into the structure.

Everything was metal – cupboards, which we've still got, and of course the window frames, which were terrible because they rusted however much you painted them. Then they put wooden ones in and now we've had those replaced. And we've still got the original iron bath. They came to fit a plastic one and the man said there's nothing wrong with your iron bath, you're mad if you have it taken out, so we left it in.

The house was heated by a black 'Siesta' vitreous enamelled coke-fired stove – made by Newton Chambers. But it didn't burn well with coke and you had to resort to a coal fire. And the snag was that with burning coal the bottoms soon burnt out and had to be replaced about every six or seven months. Now we have electric fires. People who have come and gone from the prefabs here have complained about them being cold but we've never come across that. The Siesta stove had a stovepipe clad around with a steel fabrication and the heat from that fed into two ducts, one in each bedroom. So you had a form of central heating that way. And it heated the towel rail in the bathroom. And outside we've the original coal-place made from corrugated iron like an Anderson shelter, but not built half underground.

Percy Fullwood, born 1920

Percy and Bessie Fullwood outside 84 Steven Crescent.

Low Newbiggin

I went to live at 79 Low Newbiggin in 1949 at the age of two. Our house was one of four at the side of the pond. Our next door neighbour was Mrs Burgin and her grandson, Roy. Next door to her lived Mr and Mrs Lewis with their two sons John and Richard and round the corner in the original farmhouse lived Mr and Mrs Gum with their three adult sons.

Our house was a converted farm building and consisted of one room downstairs and one up. The upstairs room was divided by a hardboard partition to make a small bedroom in which I slept with my sister. The room downstairs had a very large pantry which went the complete length of the house and had a stone slab at one end with large meat hooks in the ceiling. The floor was stone paving and not at all even. We had one cold water tap above a very shallow stone sink. We had a brick built boiler for heating water and a black leaded fireplace with an oven at one side, the fire in the middle, and a boiler again for heating water at the other side. All the cooking was done in this oven and on the hob, the only addition for pans or the kettle was a primus stove. Flat irons were also heated on the hob when the ironing needed doing. Our room was lit by a large tilly lamp hung from the ceiling. Lighting upstairs consisted of small tilly lamps which you took with you. Toilets were earth toilets and these were round the side of the house.

Our entertainment was largely home made: hop scotch, whip and top and five stones in summer. We had a radio with an accumulator and a wind-up gramophone but very few records. We also had a pedal organ which mum had had since she was nine years old, so many winter evenings were spent singing.

Janet Womersley (left), her sister Pat, and mother, Doreen, outside their cottage at 79 Low Newbiggin.

Janet Haddock (née Womersley), born 1946

Bracken Hill Camp

My first memories are of walking along Sheringham Road with my mother and being told that we would soon be moving there. That was in 1950 and I was three years old. We moved into 70 Sheringham Road in March of that year. It was one of three roads on what was always called

Bracken Hill Camp. Originally built as an Army camp the site was also used to house evacuated Dutch children towards the end of the war. It was then taken over by Wortley Rural District Council as temporary housing.

The houses were all the same – semi-detached, one-storey buildings with corrugated iron roofs, known as hostels. On entering the side door a long corridor stretched ahead. On the left was the only bedroom, shared between my parents, myself and later my baby sister, Jane. This room had a small stove used for heating the bedroom in winter. It produced so much heat that the furniture was often in danger of scorching. Next was the living/dining room, complete with Aga-style range, which served for both heating and cooking. The metal-framed windows had many cracked panes which dad used to seal up with chewing gum to stop the wind whistling through. Just past the living room the corridor widened to form a small kitchen area with sink and cupboards. The corridor ended with a Welsh dresser which housed the plates and dishes. There was a small bathroom and toilet with cast-iron bath and metal sink. Mother was the practical one. She decorated the walls using wallpaper of two different patterns, separated with a coloured border. The wallpaper used to come with edges which needed trimming. I used to pin the long, curly paper trimmings into my straight hair to produce ringlets.

Carol Limb (née Adams), born 1946

Margot (left) and Pat Hirst on one of their regular family walks.

Family Sundays

We lived in Church Street, Ecclesfield in the 1950s, and Sundays for our family were all very much the same. After breakfast it would be out for a walk with dad, who would take us and also quite a few of our friends. He always ended up carrying everyone's coats as we all grew hot with running around. Grandad and Uncle Joe would go to Ecclesfield Working Men's Club and say they were going to the chapel (which, at the time, we believed).

Whilst we were out my mother would cook the dinner, which in our house was always roast beef and Yorkshire pudding. Every Sunday afternoon we had to go to Ecclesfield Church Sunday School and then in the evening, after tea, (weather permitting) the whole family would go out for a walk. Very often, Auntie Mabel and Uncle Joe, who only lived two doors away, would also come. Auntie Mabel wore a brown felt hat and

Uncle Joe, Margot and I would gather 'sticky bobs' and throw them very gently onto the back of it as she was walking until a big bunch had gathered. She would walk home like that, knowing nothing about what we had been up to.

Auntie Mabel was quite a regular churchgoer at the time and finally, after much bullying and cajoling, managed to persuade Uncle Joe to go to church with her one Sunday. Alas, as it happened, the vicar in his sermon referred to 'the local froth blowers' and Uncle Joe said he was looking straight at him! Needless to say, that put a very abrupt end to uncle's church going!

Pat Evans (née Hirst), born 1937

Almost all the contributions in this book are by people looking back over the century. However, some local residents kept diaries and recorded things as they happened. Hugh Hirst of Ecclesfield, a deputy at Smithy Wood, kept very detailed diaries for the years 1958 and 1959. Do you remember the heatwave of 1959? This is how Hugh Hirst recorded that glorious summer:

Phew! What a Scorcher!

Monday 8 June:
Fine and clear today. I think it's going to be a nice summer.

Wednesday 10 June:
Flaming June and here it is. Everybody sweltering in the heat.

Sunday 14 June:
Winnie and I took a bus to Thurgoland and had a walk round Low Thurgoland and Wortley Station. Lovely evening.

Friday 19 June:
Nice warm day today. We could do with a shower of rain but after all the summers we've had we had better enjoy the sun whilst it's here.

Saturday 20 June:
Ah! rained during the night (the first time for nine days) but not for long.

Monday 22 June:
Fine and sunny in fact hot. My week's holiday. Started on the front bedroom. Never saw light of day today; worked until 10.15 p.m.

Wednesday 24 June:
Hotter than ever (if it's possible). Finished front bedroom. Ceiling white, walls columbine, windows and doors white, fireplace white and columbine; going to do the top in the kitchen tonight. Oh! I forgot, the wall over the fireplace is papered in sweet pea paper. Total cost £5 9s 1d. Labour nowt!

Saturday 4 July:
What a scorcher! Not a cloud in the sky all day; at Barnsley 91° was recorded.

Thursday 23 July:
A real old fashioned summer's day, starting with a little mist in the morning and then the sun came out and beat upon us mercilessly. Max [his dog] and Shane [a friend's border collie] enjoyed a run and a splash on the Shroggs.

Friday 24 July:
I see a number of fields of corn have already been cut. This is really early but of course it's been such a warm, dry summer.

Sunday 26 June:
Peter has been helping Joe [Cuthbert at

Hugh Hirst and companion outside Ecclesfield church.

Whitley] to get the [steam] engines ready for threshing.

Wednesday 29 July:
By gum, it's warm.

Monday 10 August:
Warm but very dull, looks as though it could rain any minute. Fetched $2\frac{1}{2}$lbs dwarf beans from garden and cooked them along with some new potatoes and bacon and had them for supper – delicious.

Wednesday 19 August:
Peter went threshing up Alec [Elliott] Lane with Cuthberts. I took some photos; it was a smashing day; we are in the middle of a heatwave.

Saturday 22 August:
A proper scorcher.

Monday 24 August:
I think everybody would welcome a nice few hours of rain if it was only to cool things down a bit and wash the drains out. I never remember a summer as hot and dry as this although 1926 wasn't a bad one.

Monday 31 August-Thursday 3 September:
Nothing to report except the weather is hot, hot, HOT!

Tuesday 8 September:
Another scorcher. Greno Wood's on fire. This is about 7 p.m., 8.15 p.m. just one blazing inferno about a mile long.

Wednesday 9 September:
The air is full of smoke. Greno Wood has been burning all night even though two fire brigades are in constant attendance; you see there is very little water.

Friday 11 September:
Just a repetition of the last few months on the weather report. Warm, very warm, hot, stuffy, heavy, stifling, unbearable and the water situation is getting really serious especially in the western counties such as Devon and Cornwall.

Monday 21 September:
Cloudy and cool today, looks as though we are heading for rain.

Tuesday 22 September:
Not on your life; it is fine again this morning and plenty of sunshine too!

Wednesday 30 September:
Glorious day as regards the sun, but everyone is really needing rain. Stockport has only 16 days' supply.

Saturday 3 October:
What a scorcher! Do you know it's reached almost 80° in Sheffield today.
DON'T FORGET TO PUT THE CLOCK BACK TONIGHT.

Wednesday 7 October:
Summer's day. Want to know 'owt else? Well, it's Wednesday.

Monday 12 October:
At long last it is raining steadily this morning and what a welcome it really is. Rained until about 8.30 p.m. and then cleared up; now it is moonlight and a clear sky.

John William Cuthbert and his son Joe on their steam threshing engine on Penistone Road, Grenoside, 1958.

Wednesday 21 October:
Sunny this morning with a good strong wind, a delight to be outside, in fact Max went out with me all morning (4 hrs). Went to Sheffield on train and then to Hippodrome, *Jack the Ripper*.

Thursday 22 October:
Went out again all morning with Max; grand morning with a stiff breeze. I see all the fields around here are picked clean of potatoes (taty pickin' week).

Friday 13 November:
Bitterly cold and raining. We seem to have plunged from SUMMER into the very depth of WINTER. Winnie's got a ticket for the Lyceum to see *The Dancing Years* tonight.

Hugh Hirst, born 1909

Albert Turton with his trusty walking stick.

Uncle Albert

I remember my Uncle Albert (Turton) with affection. He was born in 1905 and died in 1995. He was the second son of Arthur and Elizabeth Turton and spent his early childhood living up 'The Gang' on Townend Road, Ecclesfield. In later years he moved onto Greaves Road. He never married and spent his working life first as a farm labourer and then at Hall and Pickles. He loved walking and was a keen follower of the Ecclesfield Beagles. On his walks he visited friends and collected all sorts of bits and pieces 'in case they were needed'. Over the years his spine began to curve and he was almost doubled over to a point where if you passed him in your car he would just raise his head a little to see your registration number, and as he knew all the registration numbers of his friends and acquaintances, he would raise his hand as you passed.

At the age of about eighty-four he had to go into hospital after a fall and he was given a new walking stick. Suddenly he seemed to be standing much straighter than he had done for years. He then told us that every time his old wooden walking stick wore through a ferrule, instead of having a new one fitted he would saw the end off the stick. Over the years the stick had become shorter and he had stooped further!

Shirley Kirk (née Watkinson), born 1953

CHAPTER 2

Village Life

Chambers' grocery and wine and spirits store and sub-post office, Wortley Road, High Green.

High Green Town Crier

My grandfather, George Moorhouse, who was always known as 'Captain', was the last town crier in High Green. He lived in a cottage at the bottom of Piece End and was a miner. When there was going to be anything special like a gala or club trip grandad used to go round with a big handbell shouting, 'Oyez! Oyez! Please take notice.' He didn't wear any special clothes but I remember seeing him, carrying his bell, walking up the fields from Piece End to Potter Hill. He retired in the 1920s and gave his handbell to High Green Working Men's Club.

Connie Ellis (née Moorhouse), born 1915

High Green Memories

When I came to live at The Poplars, at the bottom of Thompson Hill, at the age of fourteen (in 1925) I only moved across the road from 9 Westwood Road, where I was born. Over the fence at the bottom of our garden was Gore's orchard, including a tennis court in the far corner. Mr Gore kept Angram Bank Farm. The farmlands are now part of Angram Bank housing estate. I remember when all the land was pasture. I used to gather milkmaids on a Sunday morning after chapel on my way to visit Auntie Re in Mortomley. We had a wash house (now our outhouse) where my gran used to brew stout in the set pot.

We had a weekly visit from a man selling oatcakes and pikelets, rag and bone men galore and an old Jew who carried all sizes of glass on his back came to repair windows. The tingalary man was a regular visitor and when he left his street organ in the slaughter house of the local butcher over the weekend we used to have fun with it! When I was very little there used to be a Friday market almost opposite the Market Inn. I wasn't very old when it finished. Further up Wortley Road was the post office kept by a schoolmarm-ish lady called Chambers. Funerals were different then. Today's funerals are the 'all-in' variety, but when I was young the bearers were 'called' by the person or persons who laid out the body. Usually they would be friends or workmates of the deceased and it was normally white ties for women and black ties for men, plus gloves. Grandpa Lawton was greatly in demand for the job.

Clara Housley (née Marshall), born 1911

Jim Crow '...waited for one train going to Sheffield and rode with the engine driver and fireman who fed it bits.'

Jim Crow

It would be about 1917, the First World War, and food was in very short supply due to the sinking of ships by the German submarines, and we had no tame rabbits big enough to eat. There was a rookery at Westwood Station and the young rooks were perched on the boughs of the trees learning to fly, so we made catapults to knock them off, as they had nice tender breasts and lovely in a pie. One rook had a damaged wing and couldn't fly, so I took it home and put it in a little box in the fender by the side of the fire. We gave it bits of food and it became very tame and it could say quite a lot of words and would fly on chairs and even on the table when it was hungry and say, 'Come on then.' It became known as Jim Crow. It liked any kind of fat, lard, etc. But it made such a mess and began to break things so my dad put it outside and shut the door. It became a playmate of all us children. It had a very big, black, long beak and gave the cats and dogs a swipe if they went near its food. It

The master's house at Grenoside Workhouse.

would knock at doors with its beak but only a few would let it in.

It liked trains and every day it flew back to the station where it was hatched and the porters and stationmaster fed it. Most days it waited for one train going to Sheffield and rode with the engine driver and fireman who fed it bits. It always dropped off at Brightside Station where it became a showpiece with the staff. It always caught the same train and driver on its way back to Barnsley and always dropped off at Westwood Station. Its favourite perch was on the station gatepost and as you went through the gate it would say, 'Hello, come on then,' and it made you jump if you hadn't seen it. If it knew you, it would try and ride on your head or shoulder. One day, however, it didn't come back from one of its trips to Brightside.

Colin Sansam, born 1915

Grenoside Workhouse

The land now occupied by Grenoside Council offices used to be the workhouse gardens and was worked by the permanent inmates of the institution. They wore grey fustian trousers and jackets and worked hard and kept the ground well planted and tidy. The food produced was used to feed the inmates of the workhouse and the fever hospital above the workhouse. At that time there was a large number of inmates – children of unknown parentage, orphans, aged people and people who were too proud to ask for what was then known as parish relief. This was the only source from which help could come before the First World War. The men working in the gardens were allowed a copper or two for spending money and if they had relatives have a day off on Sunday to visit them and spend their pocket money. Sometimes on Saturday morning they would ask me to go on to Womersley's shop for twopennyworth of tobacco. I would sometimes have five or six lots for which in turn they gave me a penny for fetching it. Sometimes they would slip me a cabbage or cauliflower over the wall, to which the foreman turned a blind eye.

Connected to the workhouse was what was known as the vagrancy ward. This was the part of the buildings that housed the tramps that travelled in those days from one place to another. Our cottage wall to which the chimney was attached faced the footpath. The wall was warm and in winter the tramps would stand against the wall waiting for the bell which was rung at 6 p.m. They would then hurry up the lane to the vagrancy ward, there to be signed in and examined by the workhouse master and his helpers, after which they received a pot of tea, something to eat and a bed.

Next morning at 6 a.m. the bell would ring again. They were got up, made to wash, given something to eat and drink and then those that were able had to break two barrowfuls of cinders that came from Thorncliffe Ironworks into pieces about the size of an apple. These were used to repair roads before the use of tar macadam. When first laid they left the road very rough, alright for horses in the winter but not so in summer when they wore the horses shoes out and hurt their feet.

Arthur Andrews, born 1900

Birth and Death at Westwood

Old Mrs Mallion acted as midwife and I don't remember any crippled or deformed babies being born. It was generally accepted that if you survived the first year you stood a good chance of living the next seventy, barring accidents. And accidents there were in plenty, particularly in the male population, usually as a result of working down Tankersley Pit. Men were old at fifty, lungs clogged with coal dust or crippled by accidents at work.

Funerals created a diversion for us young ones. There was a big funeral coach, usually pulled by three huge black Belgian horses, with the corpse being slid into a special place under the driver's seat and the mourners riding in the body of the coach behind the coffin.

The usual custom after any death was to lay out the corpse in the front room and any neighbours who wished to do so could visit and view the body. On one such occasion, the wife having died in hospital and brought home in the coffin on the morning of the funeral, all the relatives and friends gathered waiting for the coach to come. The coffin was opened for inspection and the husband came out and said 'do's off, they've brought t' wrong un back'. And they had too, the corpse was that of a perfect stranger!

Len Sansam

Bookie's Runner

It was my mother and her neighbour who used to bet. Occasionally, if there was a good race and her particular jockey was on, they'd bet on the jockey. They only used to have sixpence each way. It was an offence to be betting on horses off the racecourse. I used to have to go with these sixpences to an old man who lived on the corner of Piece End, and I put the money on for them. There was only one policeman in High Green – PC Dolby, and he probably wouldn't have noticed me scuttling in and out of this old man's house with the money! My mother and her neighbour always won when they bet on a particular jockey; they didn't know anything about horses. Horses were something that pulled carts. They bet on the jockey Lester Piggott; they followed him from his first win when he was fourteen. They bet on Lester every time he showed his face in the *Daily Herald*. They always won at least half a crown, which was the dinner money for the rest of the week!

Irene Mulligan (nèe Harris), born 1929

Tally Ho!

In the winter of our first year on Thackery Row when hare hunting was prevalent in the villages around Ecclesfield, the beagles, under Tom Barlow, the huntsman, arrived in the village having walked up from the Shroggs. The dogs were put into a stable or shed while the huntsmen went into the pub for a pint. I would have been about five years old and my friend, Willis, and I wanted to look at the dogs. After one or two attempts, between us we managed to get the peg from the hasp that was holding the door. The moment we saw the dogs alright, we were covered with them and off they went all over the village with the huntsman blowing his horn and all the followers yelling. Willis and I ran to the Angel Inn football ground. If there had been a hare there we should have caught it the speed we went at. It was a mystery for a long time how those hounds got out, perhaps until now!

Arthur Andrews, born 1900

Chapeltown, 1920s

Many houses had gardens where families grew their own food – potatoes, beans, peas, cabbage – and some would have an allotment garden. Some families kept a few fowls to provide eggs and in some cases a pig was reared. If I told you that on Saturday mornings many children took drugs you would be shocked. But don't be, the drugs in question were just wooden boxes mounted on a pair of old pram wheels, with handles attached to the box. They were used on Saturday mornings to shop at the Co-op on Station Road. You see, baking bread twice a week for a large family, plus feed for maybe six hens, meant shopping for a lot of flour and chicken feed – no cars – hence the drugs to carry the groceries home. The flour and chicken bran were kept in an upstairs room at the Co-op and came to shop level down a metal chute. The shop assistant placed a bag over the bottom of the chute and collected the estimated amount and then weighed it. Sugar and tea was also weighed and put into bags. If you wanted a pound of butter or lard two flat wooden blades were used to cut it from a large block and then shape it before it was weighed and wrapped. Cheese was cut with a wire with a handle on each end.

Although we had some good doctors, Dr Sands and Dr Barraclough in Chapeltown and Dr Norton in Mortomley, there was no health service and home cures were often used. A sprain was soaked in hot water and comfrey leaves, a bad chest was rubbed in goose grease or covered with a bread or bran poultice, and many children took cod liver oil or drank hyssop tea to keep away colds.

Eddie Ogle, born 1914

Chapeltown Co-op, Station Road.

Westwood Rows, originally built to house blackleg labour during the lockout at Newton Chambers' collieries in 1869-70.

Newcomers to Westwood Rows

Grenosiders, who had worked at Oughtibridge Pit, and had practically worked out the ganister mines, started working at Tankersley Colliery and Wharncliffe Silkstone Pit from around 1912. As houses on the Westwood Rows became vacant they were given to Grenoside miners who had come to work at Tankersley because they knew they were good workmen and prepared to accept the conditions as they were and the wages they paid for the simple reason that they hadn't any money. There was friction on the Rows at first and there were some there who thought they owned the houses. In about 1915 our family was given a house there. We were like invaders going into an establishment that had been settled for some time. The residents had their own ways and they didn't like new methods or new faces being introduced and there were conflicts, terrible conflicts, between us. They wouldn't let us play with their children or let us play on the football field and they'd do everything possible to cause disruption. There were fights, mostly between women, usually about children. Now and again men got a fight up if the women goaded them into it. One day the women had been on to Mrs Hawksworth and her children and they'd been having a grand do so she waited while they'd all got settled down for the night and she went out with the prop and broke all their windows! She quietened them alright! Eventually we got as we were all friendly, the war and its shortages, the atmosphere of fear and loss brought us together.

One source of recreation and pleasure was Westwood dam. Besides providing good fishing for local anglers we enjoyed it for swimming in (much to the annoyance of the anglers). We would come home from work at the pit, drop our pit clothes off, put on our bathing trunks and take soap and a towel and dive in. It was the only bath we got unless we went up to High Green Working Men's Club and paid twopence for a bath on Saturdays.

Arthur Andrews , born 1900

Thorncliffe Avenue, 1920s

We lived at the side of the roadway to Lane End in the short row of houses. They were all two-up and two-down with a stone sink in the kitchen and only cold running water. Nearby and more or less in front of the houses was a pond or dam fed by the Charlton Brook. The roadway was private and owned by Newton Chambers. It closed once a year to all traffic for twenty-four hours otherwise it would no longer be private and could be taken over by Wortley Rural District Council. My mother used to take the tolls from the hawkers with their horses and drays and the occasional lorry or van that came along. For this she received three shillings a week. There were often times when she hadn't taken much during the week so she returned the three shillings as tolls taken. It was a job that she never wanted, but I think it went with the house.

Most of our neighbours had an allotment where they grew their own vegetables and potatoes. We had an allotment and we also kept hens so we were never short of eggs. We fetched most of our groceries from Warren Co-op. It was often my job to fetch them using a home-made drug.

In the 1920s the seasons seemed distinct. Winter was very cold with plenty of snow

Thorncliffe Avenue with the dam fed by Charlton Brook and some of the nearby allotments.

and frost. The dam was frozen over from the end of December through to March. Skating was a regular feature for grown ups and I've seen fires lit in an old oil drum with holes punched in and stood on three bricks on the ice so that they could go and warm themselves. Sledging was a favourite pastime with us young ones. We used to sledge in a field up Lane End. From behind Lound Girls' School the field had a good slope down to the brook in the bottom. On Sunday evenings in the spring and summer we would get dressed up in our best clothes and be taken for a walk by our parents. We usually ended up in Chapeltown Park where we would sit with our parents to listen to one of the local brass bands playing in the bandstand.

Charles Baines, born 1920

Wallet End, Ecclesfield

In the 1920s the area around the parade of shops on High Street now called 'Ecclesfield Centre' was known as Wallet End. The present fish and chip shop occupies the same building today as it did at least seventy years ago. The small building to the left was a cobbler's shop kept for many years by Mr Goodison who walked round the area delivering boots and shoes to his customers. On Sundays he taught small children in Sunday school and was a very respected member of the community. The other side of the chip shop was a one-room residence lived in by a man called Gregory. A feature of most of the cottages in The Wallet were the wooden shutters which were hinged to the downstairs windows and folded back to the walls. When darkness fell they would be swung over the windows for warmth and protection. A narrow sunken lane known as T'owd Lane or Icky Picky Lane ran from The Wallet to Knowle Top and probably served the quarry there. An old man called Rushby lived in a hut in the quarry for some years and constructed a simple tennis court in the hope of earning some income, but it was not a success. He did make a bit of money selling nettle beer. Adjoining the quarry was a spring which flowed into a stone trough. The quarry and spring were situated roughly at the top of Tunwell Avenue.

One of the most important and oldest large houses in The Wallet was the home of the Green family who owned the iron foundry on Station Road. It was where the old Co-operative stores stand. Opposite the Greyhound Hotel was a group of extremely old cottages known as the Low Fold. In front of Bank House (now The Regency restaurant) were two cottages with the downstairs rooms below the level of the road. Each had a flight of stone steps leading down to a side door. One of them was a shop kept by Mrs Wrigley who subsequently became Mrs Parker. She sold sweets and comics. I used to buy *Comic Cuts* and when I was older the *Magnet* which featured Harry Wharton and Billy Bunter and the rest of the boys of Greyfriars School. The shop window was very small and low, the bottom

The Sportsman Inn (now demolished) at Wallet End, Ecclesfield.

being level with the pavement and you had to bend down to look in. A farmhouse known as Shaw's Farm stood next to the Greyhound. It was a large farm producing milk and cereal and root crops. Birds such as the corncrake nested in the fields and on a summer's evening the nightjar's call could be heard. Another vivid memory is of the swifts, swallows and house martins which used to swarm in their hundreds around the Wesleyan Methodist chapel.

Another house at Wallet End was Gipsy Frank's house. He kept hens which were allowed to wander in and out of the house as they pleased as the door always seemed to be open. In a workshop behind the old Co-op building one of the Ridge family produced gimlets. Another member of the Ridge family forged augers in a workshop between the Ball Inn and the Greyhound Hotel. An old building which always interested me was Singleton's Farm, now, I believe, a transport firm. The only transport in my day consisted of one horse and a two-wheeled cart engaged in carrying coal, coke and pig iron from the station yard to Green's Foundry and Parker's File Cutting Works.

Joseph Knott, born 1915

Mr Walton, steward, at the back of High Green Working Men's Club.

Like Father Like Son

Elaine was telling me about her brother Jimmy going scrumping. He was gathering all the pears in the orchard at St Mary's presbytery when he looked up and saw Father Reynolds.

He said 'Right young Jimmy, just you wait till I see your dad!' And Jimmy said 'Mi dad's up t' tree Father!'

Margaret O'Toole (née Rice), born 1930

High Green WMC

Between 1935 and 1952 High Green Working Men's Club was my home; I was two years old when we went there and in my second year at university when my father retired. All his earlier working life he had been employed as a coal hewer in the local pits but his trade union activities in the 1920s caused him to be blacklisted by the local pit managers and he had been out of work for about three years before his appointment as steward. Luckily, and not surprisingly, considering his political

Billiards and Snooker Room, High Green Working Men's Club.

commitments and his keen interest in discussion and debate, he very much enjoyed his new job, relishing the company and conversation of working men.

When we lived at the club it had four medium-sized rooms, a very large room, two urinals (as the men's toilets were then called), a bar and a small reception room – all on the ground floor. Upstairs there was a roomy concert room and underneath the club were two cellars.

The reading room was squarish, well-lit by large sash windows and made cosy in long winter evenings by a coal fire. In here there were comfortable chairs around two large rectangular tables – perfect for spreading out newspapers and magazines. Above one table and for most of the length of one wall was a dark-wood, glass-fronted bookcase housing a small library. A wide range of newspapers was delivered every day and several weekly or monthly magazines. I well remember the *National Geographic*, the *Illustrated London News* and *Hansard* being always there. One of the functions of such a club was to provide opportunities for working men to keep abreast of current affairs and to develop wider reading and varied interests.

The long games room had half a dozen or so smallish rectangular tables for playing cards, dominoes and other table games. There was padded seating along two walls and there were stools around the tables. The 'best room', named so I imagine because it boasted the most comfortable seating (padded seats running right round the walls, and chairs with arm supports), was also provided with a radio. It was a comfortable, relaxing room with small round tables placed for easy conversation and, certainly in the evenings, warmed by a coal fire. I remember men sitting in here listening to the 'wireless' in the early evening, quiet and content in the firelight, choosing not yet to put on the lights. Here, too, men gathered together to listen to important news about the progress of the Second World War or share favourite programmes. The very large room on the ground floor was used for playing billiards and snooker. It had padded seats for spectators along the long walls, two full-sized tables and a beautiful, polished, wood-block floor – not to be scratched.

A wide staircase immediately facing the front door went up to the concert room which had a stage, a piano and lots of small round tables and comfortable chairs. Saturday night was entertainment night and looked forward to by many wives. I remember the noise of people talking, laughing, singing and the beat of music and some tunes I knew coming through the bedroom walls. I don't think the noise disturbed me – it was a kind of company and I was used to it. Much later, of course, came bingo.

Two cellars ran beneath the whole frontage of the building. The beer and wine cellar led down from the bar and had a cool, concrete floor and wooden racks to support the barrels and store the wines and spirits. All draught beer was tapped and hand-pumped up to the bar. I was old enough to serve in the bar for about a year before we left and I was warned by several of the customers (joking I am sure!) not to serve them a 'cuckoo'. The idea was to have value for money and therefore as little froth as possible on top of the beer was a requirement; a 'cuckoo' was too much froth.

The other cellar was approached from the kitchen and had two compartments: one housed the coke boiler and coke, coal and wood for fires and was very warm; the

Ecclesfield Hospital Parade Band, 1911.

smaller area was for general storage but during the war became our air-raid shelter. We had mattresses and blankets down there and during the two big raids on Sheffield (high explosives on a Thursday night and incendiary bombs on the following Sunday night) we slept warm and safe down there. On the Monday morning I remember the sky over Sheffield was a red haze.

Pat Cunningham (née Walton), born 1933

Ecclesfield Village Characters

Every village had its pig killer who made a living by going round slaughtering the cottage pigs. Many people kept a pig which was fed on swill. This feed consisted of potato peelings and bread crusts, etc., collected from neighbours and boiled in an old cast iron copper and mixed with meal before being fed to the pig. For their contributions the neighbours were given odd bits when the pig was slaughtered. 'Owd Drib' used to march round the village in a blue and white striped smock adorned with a thick leather belt from which hung various sharp knives and tools that he used to ply his trade. The pigs were slaughtered in a convenient backyard, roped down to a strong wooden frame called a block. The squeals were horrendous and everyone knew that everything from the pig was used except the squeal.

Joe Jubb will perhaps be remembered by some for his conducting of Ecclesfield Brass Band which he carried out with his eyes shut tightly and his right foot turned at a right angle to his left, tapping out the beat. On occasions he also acted as town crier. Various characters visited the village from time to time selling their wares or services. One of these was a Jew who mended windows and carried the glass on a wooden frame on his back. He used to knock on doors and enquire of any 'Vindows to mend'. A man selling pots came fairly frequently, carrying them on a basket on his head. He had a thick pad stitched on top of his cap for comfort. Others who carried a load on their head were the oatcake and pikelet man and a man selling shellfish. Another vendor who came every Saturday with a horse and dray was the greengrocer, Ernest Hastings, equipped with a stentorian voice; he could be heard for miles.

Joseph Knott, born 1915

Newbiggin

In 1949 I arrived at the hamlet of Low Newbiggin with my wife, Doreen, and two daughters, Janet and Pat. Low Newbiggin consisted of four cottages in one block and another cottage which stood on its own by the roadside. The cottages were leased by Newton Chambers from Earl Fitzwilliam. I worked for Newton Chambers and the rent of 4s 11d per week was stopped out of my wages by the firm. At the side of our cottage was Newbiggin Pond and opposite, on the edge of the wood, was the colliery pumping station, worked by steam. Outside the boiler room was a very large galvanised tank always full of boiling water, so washdays and bath nights were never a problem.

The old lady who lived at the back of us was quite a character. She had a husband and three sons and each one left for work at a different time. In order to wake each one at the appropriate time she would ring a large handbell at the bottom of the stairs. They rose alright and so did everyone else in

Newbiggin Cottages at the turn of the twentieth century.

the cottages. The sons grew tired of the bell and threw it into the pond. Shortly after, she was given an old bugle, what a piercing screech!

Life could be rather grim in the winter. Once after heavy rain the pond flooded and the water filled our coal-shed. I brought a shovel full of coal into the house only to find scores of tiny frogs among the coals, and we had quite a hectic time catching them in the living room.

Once a large grass snake came into the house and caused a stir. Summer was a great time. I used to rise at four o'clock to hear the dawn chorus and see the foxes heading back to their dens. In season there was plenty to eat – rabbits, partridge, pheasant and the occasional duck. Rabbit pie with thick onion gravy was always a family favourite. I once watched a weasel empty a blackbird's nest of four fledglings and eat them. When it was warm and sunny we would take our tea into the field at the side of the pond and have a good natter with the neighbours.

Herbert Womersley, born 1920

New Street Childhood

I grew up in New Street in the 1950s. I thought it was a daft name – even then it was one of the oldest parts of the village. Granny Walton, who lived in the next to the top house, remembered it being built.

We lived next door to the Colton family, staunch Methodists, who attended Wortley Road chapel. Living across the other side was one of my favourite people, Mrs Christina 'Chrissie' Matthewman. She kept a few fowls, and when I was ill with scarlet fever she brought me a few eggs. These were still on ration and difficult to get in the shops. Chrissie was not well off but she always refused any kind of payment. She once told me that she had never seen the sea, and had never ridden in a train. The Matthewmans owned a friendly black and white dog of indeterminate breed. His name was Roger and he was very fond of ice cream. Every Sunday afternoon Simpson's ice cream cart would come down New Street. Roger would be given a threepenny bit, which he held in his mouth whilst waiting in the queue. When his turn came, he would jump up and drop his money on the serving hatch. Mr Simpson would make him a cornet which would rapidly disappear, accompanied by loud, slurping noises of enjoyment. Today he would probably be filmed by a TV station.

Next to the Matthewmans lived Mr and Mrs Dransfield. I was very proud when one of their daughters named her baby Susan. I was sure the little girl had been named after me! Near the bottom of New Street lived Mrs Hannah Mellor, the street's unofficial, and usually unpaid, nurse and adviser. Any sort of crisis would find Mrs Mellor in attendance. Mums would consult her if their children were ill. She also acted as emergency midwife, almost delivering me, as I am told the midwife made it with only minutes to spare.

At the top of New Street stood Sellar's Row, a terrace of three cottages older than New Street itself. In the first two lived the Cottons and the Yales. Mrs Daisy Yale had been a Cotton. In the end cottage lived Mr and Mrs 'Teddy' Bradbury. Mrs Bradbury had a rather harsh Glaswegian accent but was a lovely lady. Mr Bradbury was somewhat irascible. If your ball, or anything else, went into 'Owd' Bradbury's garden, you were wise to consider it lost.

A perpetual state of war existed between the children of New Street and those of adjacent Piece End. It was a very brave, or

New Street, when it was really new.

very foolish, New Streeter who ventured alone down Piece End. Fists and sometimes stones would bombard the hapless trespasser. One evening I was sent to 'Becca's' shop to buy some bread. Following a cry of 'New Streeter' I was chased all the way home by an irate and fast Piece Ender, dropping most of my bread on the way. I salvaged what I could, but my father got very grey sandwiches for his snap the next day!

Susan Kelsall (née Cuckson), born 1946

Territorialism

I was born and bred in Grenoside and it seems that there are people, and I am no exception, who feel that Grenoside is the only place on earth that God has touched, and to be a true Grenosider you have to be born in the village or have lived there for 150 years.

A school friend of mine, I'll call him Barry, was playing in a football match between Ecclesfield and Grenoside. The match took place on the football field behind the Angel Inn on Main Street in the mid-1950s. Barry was sent off to get some loose studs in his boots fixed and he approached an old man standing near the field wall. They had this conversation:

Barry: 'Hello, do you live close by?'
Man: 'Tha plays fer them dun't tha?'
Barry: 'Yes, but I've to get my studs fixed, could I borrow a hammer?'
Man: 'What do the' call thee?'
Barry: 'Barry...but I've got to get my boots fixed.'
Man: 'Does tha 'ave any relatives i' Grenner?'
Barry: 'Yes, but what about my boots?'
Man: 'Weere du they live?'
Barry: 'Topside.'
Man: 'I' that case ah'll get thee t' 'ammer.'

John Rodgers, born 1937

Grenoside Bible Class Football Club, 1909.

CHAPTER 3
Schooldays

Standard 2 at Warren School in 1928. Charles Baines is third from the right on the back row.

Attending Warren School, 1920s

From about five years of age I attended Warren School and left when I was eleven in 1931. I remember one teacher in particular, Mrs Turner who was very handy with a thin cane. I think her cane only lasted her about a fortnight. The boy who brought her a new one was often the first to sample it!

Charles Baines, born 1920

An Ecclesfield Education

When I was five in 1928 I attended Rawson's Infant School at Ecclesfield. To get there I left my home in Nether Terrace and walked through the park and up to the Lady Croft. We always stopped near the top of Lady Croft in order to spit on a diamond-shaped stone, believing it would bring us good luck!

When I was eight I moved to the Junior School. It stood behind the stone-built Boys' School, which my brother Harry attended. The Girls' School was corrugated

Standard 1 at Rawson's Infant School, Ecclesfield, 1928.

Form 3A at Ecclesfield Grammar School, 1931-32.

metal on the outside and the inside walls were stained tongue and grooved wood. I learned in later years that my maternal grandfather, Arthur Duncan, had, with a group of men, helped with the woodwork. On wet days Harry and I went across the road from school to my grandma's for a light lunch – usually a boiled egg and a cup of cocoa. Nobody could make cocoa as good as my grandma!

In September 1934 I started going to Ecclesfield Grammar School where I spent seven very happy years. Apart from lessons we had clubs after school. I learned country and ballroom dancing. I also played hockey for the school on Saturday mornings. We travelled to Wath, Woodhouse, Mexborough, and Ackworth Boarding School which was our favourite.

Doris Harrison (née France), born 1923

Lound School, 1920s

The day always started at Lound School with morning assembly in the hall where the headmaster, Mr Sawdon, made any relevant announcements, a hymn was sung and there was a reading from the bible, often by an older child. Lessons for younger children concentrated on reading, writing and learning tables for arithmetic. Older children also learned grammar, punctuation and spelling and did composition. History and geography were popular. History started at 1066 and finished in 1918 and it was basically British history. Geography was worldwide but focused on the British Empire. We had regular scripture lessons and drawing sessions. The nearest we got to science was nature study – this was popular because on

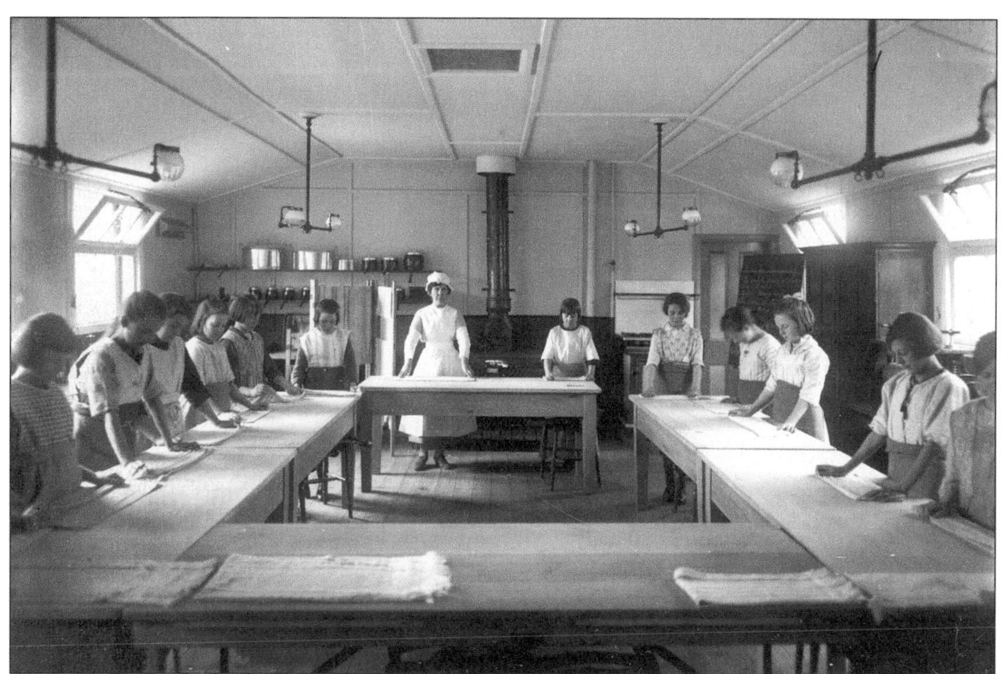

Domestic science room, Lound School, Chapeltown, 1920s.

fine summer days it could involve a walk in the woods and fields. Skylarks and corncrakes were often heard and the cuckoo heralded spring. Once a week the top class of girls and boys would crowd into one classroom, sitting three to a desk, and have a singing lesson. We also had a large wooden hut which was so constructed that one entrance was from the girls' playground and the other was from the boys' yard. The girls used their side for regular cookery lessons, while the boys had carpentry. We were fortunate at Lound School in having a large playing field and part of this was given over to gardening. We worked in pairs on a small plot of land and grew lettuce, beetroot, radishes, and potatoes. We were even allowed to take the produce home.

Eddie Ogle, born 1914

Burncross Council School

In the spring of 1929 I arrived, aged eight and a half, at Burncross Council School. I had been ill for over a year and before that had about a year at a private school where I learnt very little. I had two happy years at Burncross until I left in 1931 to go to the newly-opened Ecclesfield Grammar School.

I think the school was probably typical of its time. We received a sound basic education but no frills – for example, no books, paints or musical instruments – nothing to stimulate a child's imagination. I was put into Standard 3 with Miss Horsfield; she was an excellent teacher, very strict, but fair, and to me her word was as the word of God.

I could read anything and cope with money and weighing as I was allowed to shop and cook at home – but 'sums' were something else! Who in their right mind would try to fill a bath with a hole in it, I wondered. However, as that was what was required I soon learnt to produce the right answers. If you had your sums wrong you had to go out and stand in a line to have your hand caned. Before I learnt how to do them Miss Horsfield used to pass over me, resulting, of course, in other 'canees' going for me in the playground. However I learnt to give as good as I got and soon made friends.

When the bell was rung in the playground we had to stand in a line, silently, and walk up the dark tiled corridor, hanging up our coats, and into the classroom where we sat two at a desk in which there was an inkwell. We wrote with steel nibs. The windows were high up and unfortunately rarely opened to let in fresh air.

We had ten mental arithmetic questions every morning. The board was covered with little marks as Miss Horsfield tapped it with a pencil for us to write and to stop. If, say, you only had eight correct, you had to stay behind at four o'clock to make up the other two. I never found out how long some children stayed. We also did fractions, decimals, simple and compound interest, weights and measures. I can't remember how often we had ten spellings to take home, but I know that this exercise has helped me throughout my life.

A tedious thing was reading round the class – books were given out and everyone had to read a sentence in turn. This must have been agony for a few of the boys who couldn't read, and I doubt if they ever learnt.

Burncross School in the early years of the twentieth century.

For geography a large map of the world was unrolled, the British Empire coloured red. We did a lot of rote learning and I can still recite the peaks of the Pennines and the rivers of Yorkshire. In history Miss Horsfield would read stories about Hereward the Wake and King Alfred, which I loved. 'Nature' was an explanation of petals, sepals and stamens but this went over my head. Growing beans on blotting paper was interesting though. I suppose we must have done scripture but I can't recall this. 'Penmanship' (writing practice) was done on lined paper, as was composition, usually on a set subject.

Two afternoons I dreaded: one when an object was placed on a small table and we were all issued with a pencil and a piece of plain white paper. This was drawing and I hadn't the least idea how to start. I still can't draw! The other was knitting – long striped scarves, only you never got your own back the next week, so far from learning to knit I was put off it for many years.

We sang songs – now that I did enjoy – such as *The British Grenadiers* – and learnt a lot of poetry by rote. As I never saw it written down I often made mistakes, for instance, in 'Tyger, tyger burning bright' I rendered 'thy immortal symmetry' as 'cemetery' which, after all, I passed four times a day. Yes, we went home to dinner at twelve noon, there being no school meals. Since there was no traffic in those days this was quite safe and our parents would never have thought of coming to the school. There was school milk at this date, free for those who could not pay.

After Standard 3 I went to Miss Denton in Standard 4 and then had about two terms in Standard 5 with Mr Platts, the headmaster, of whom I was terrified. Thanks to him, however, seventeen of us went to Ecclesfield Grammar School.

Marian Barraclough, born 1921

Rivalry

St Mary's RC School and High Green School were great rivals. They used to call us 'Catholic Bogies' and we used to call them 'High Green Bulldogs'. We used to chase each other and fight and although our school was smaller we stayed on until we were fourteen and they finished at eleven, so we'd got the bigger ones.

Margaret O'Toole (née Rice), born 1930

Ecclesfield Boys' School

I had a lot of friends about my age – Bernard and George Ridge, Russell and Frank Heeley, the Hemmingfield brothers, Cyril Justice, Colin Whitham, Ronnie Ridge, Mick Smith, Tommy Sorsby – and my closest pal, Alan Sharp. We attended the school in Ecclesfield, on the High Street. Our teachers then were Gaffer Hawkes (headmaster), Mr Woodhead (the music teacher), Dicky Phillips, Mr MacKie and others. They were nice to us, but strict. Mr MacKie had a cane which was different from most others as it was short, thick and knobbly at the end. I felt it once (deservedly), when a gang of us, one summer evening climbed onto the roof of the school and rang the bell loudly at about six o'clock.

Of course we were identified as that gang off Strawberry and Tunwell. It was a large bell and all the village heard it and Bobby Furness

Ecclesfield Boys' School on the High Street, with its distinctive bellcote. It was built in 1894 and demolished in 1998.

Class II, St Mary's Roman Catholic School, 1919.

who lived on Yew Lane got to know and investigated. Now, there was a man who knew how to maintain discipline with teenagers!

Lewis Burrows, born 1927

Changing Sides

My friend Dorothy's father went to High Green School on Wortley Road, and he got caned for having mud on his shoes. He had come through the woods which were very muddy. His mother said, 'Well I don't think that's fair, I'll go and see the headmaster'. But her son said 'You needn't bother, I go to the Catholics now!' And he went there for the rest of his years. His mother never knew about the transfer until later.

Margaret O'Toole (née Rice), born 1930

Early and Late

My sister and I used to call for a little boy called Michael Allred to take him to school. He lived on Thompson Hill and he was always late and it made us late and we used to get the cane. Mrs Maloney set us off nice and early and she didn't know we were getting the cane for being late.

Teresa McSloy (née Holmes), born 1936

Going to School

The journey from Howbrook to High Green school was not without incident. At first my brother, Donald, took me to school, but later I often walked to High Green by myself or accompanied my younger brother, Philip. In winter weather we were often very cold and wet. Clothes drying out on the big iron fireguard round the coal fire in the

Mrs Walker's class at High Green School, 1931-32.

classroom were a familiar sight. When there was a very high wind we were kept at home because it was difficult for a small child to keep its feet and dangerous therefore to be out, but this did not happen often. The road was rough and untarred, the narrow footpath was just packed earth between wide grass verges full of dandelions and daisies in summer. In winter's rain and winds we put our heads down and forged ahead, looking neither to right nor left.

Once into High Green we mingled with the children emerging from the streets of houses into Wortley Road where the school was. There were two danger points, one of them just before the Salutation. From a yard there a gang of small, poorly-clad boys would pour out and attack if we happened to be passing as they set off for school. They had close-cropped heads like moles, sockless feet often, in clumsy boots, short trousers below the knee, men's grey flannel trousers, chopped off and too baggy for their thin bodies, often with rents in them, and grey raggy jerseys. In a gang, with their threshing arms, kicking feet and shouted abuse, they were formidable. Worse was the Piece End gang. The gang there was led by a boy whose round face and thrusting stance I well remember but whose name escapes me. We were made late for school on occasion by this fearsome dynamic creature who spread his forces across the road to block our way and vented his furious energy in pinches, cuffs and kicks.

And so at last to school, which for me was a happy place, marred by only a few fears and sadnesses. Built solidly of blackened stone, High Green School stands on the hillside, so that the boys' playground is behind a high wall several feet above the girls' playground which was shared with the mixed infants. The playground had many areas, many separate wills contending, many groupings. At the centre of its activity was stool ball, a game I have never come across since, a mixture of rounders and cricket. The game was dominated by a small group of tough-looking girls in the top class. That was Donald's class then for in a school photo I recognise them with their chopped off hair and fringes, their 'fawce' looks. That dialect word 'fawce' conveys precisely the aggressive force these girls possessed. 'Fawce cats' was the way we described them. When we first became juniors it was as well for us to skirt the stool ball area warily for there were often noisy fights, scratching, slapping, hair-pulling and plenty of swearing too.

Just inside the main gates, which were usually kept closed, there was an area between two low walls on which the younger ones used to play 'I'm on Tom Tiddler's Ground', and between the wall of the lavatories and the iron bars, by the coal cellar steps was the place for playing 'What time is it, Mr Wolf?' Both these games gave the excitement of a chase and constant movement to keep us warm. In season, of course, there was skipping when the fawce cats took charge of the long ropes and bullied everyone else, and also the more solitary pleasures of whip and top, marbles and other games. Under the sheds where there was a long bench seat was the time-honoured place for swapping things: cigarette cards, marbles, anything there was a current craze for collecting.

Just inside the girls' entrance there was a series of iron bars, a barrier at the top of two steps. This was never empty for there was always someone, usually two, for the bars would hold no more, turning somersaults. Waving arms and legs, upside down red faces, bloomers of all colours and states of repair met one as one turned into the yard and there was much squabbling for turns. The boys jeered at us from the wall above where they bobbed up and down hanging on with difficulty to peer over the top, for it was a high wall.

Jean Huddlestone (née Kirk), born 1923

School Days and Wartime

Everyone thought that the Germans would start bombing as soon as war was declared, so all the schools were closed for six weeks. In fact there was no bombing at all for some time – the 'phony war'. At Lound Infants, my first school, we were all issued with gas masks and identity cards and had to carry them wherever we went. From time to time we had to practise putting the gas mask on, so that if any gas bombs were dropped on us we would be able to get it on quickly before the gas took effect. It was made of rubber with a sort of snout that contained a filter. It fitted very tightly round my face and smelled horrible. Putting it on soon became as routine as putting on my socks.

In September 1940, when I was seven, I moved from Lound Infants to Burncross Junior School. My teacher was Miss Horsfield, we used to call her 'Hossmuck' and she was very strict. She walked about the classroom with a heavy ebony ruler in her hand. If anyone was naughty, or not getting on with their work she would hit them hard across their knuckles. She would also hit people if she thought they were going to be naughty. I didn't get the ruler too often but I once made the mistake of sighing as she walked past my desk. It really

'From time to time we had to practise putting the gas mask on...soon it became as routine as putting on my socks.'

hurt, I didn't make that mistake again.

By this time aid raids were happening regularly, so we had practices at school to teach us what to do if there was a raid while we were there. We lined up behind the teacher in alphabetical order. She led the way out of the building across the playground into the field behind the school and down a sort of tunnel into the air-raid shelter that had been built underground at the beginning of the war. It was very dark in there, no lights, and smelled damp and fusty. The teachers had torches, but only switched them on occasionally to save the batteries. We were all very nervous and excited as we sat on bench seats. When we were all settled down we were told to put on our gas masks to get used to them. We stayed in the shelter for about half an hour with our gas masks on, reciting our tables, to keep us busy.

My sister, Carol Susan, was born in 1941, just before Christmas. I was very thrilled and excited to have a baby sister, especially since her arrival was a complete surprise to me. The first I knew was that I woke up on 16 December and Aunt Phyl was there to get me off to school and told me I had a baby sister. I was so excited I told all my friends. We had sewing that day with Mrs Senior and I told her about my new sister. She said, 'Never mind that, get on with your sewing' !

I liked sewing even though we had no choice about what we made. Mrs Senior was very strict and kept making us undo it if the stitches weren't small and neat enough. The garment we had to make was a pair of pink flannelette bloomers. We also did knitting at school although we were only eight years old. We knitted scarves and gloves for the armed forces. I have a small certificate that was given to me on Empire Day 1941 that certifies that I 'helped to provide comfort and contentment to the sailors, soldiers and airmen of the British Commonwealth, who have rallied to the cause of safeguarding freedom, justice and security.' All that from one scarf!

Because of food shortages, the government was concerned about the health of children and they decided that every child should have a bottle of milk at school every day and a teaspoonful of cod liver oil. We had our milk just before playtime in the morning. The cod liver oil was doled out before we went for dinner. I hated cod liver oil, the taste of it stayed in my mouth for hours and made me feel sick. I did everything I could to avoid it. When I was ten years old I was made cod liver oil monitor – a great day. I walked along the line of children with their spoons at the ready and poured out their dose of the stuff, but never had any myself. Some children actually liked it and licked the spoon to get the last bit, something which mystified me.

By 1944 things started to change. People began to feel that we were going to win the war. We began to see American soldiers in the village from their camp at Potter Hill. Some children used to wait at the corner of the road to call out, 'Got any gum, chum?' as they passed. They were usually rewarded, but although I longed to have some I could never quite bring myself to ask, I was very shy.

Aileen Thompson (née Bagshaw), born 1933

High Green Secondary Modern

I started my secondary education at High Green Secondary Modern School in September 1955 having left Wortley Road Junior School. Everyone in the first year attended the annexe at Bracken Hill. I used to walk from High Green to Bracken Hill every day with my friends, returning home at teatime. Miss Bennett was head of school and Mr Hogg was my form teacher. I played in the school netball team and the first year passed very quickly.

My second and the subsequent three years were spent at Greengate Lane in the main school. Mr Frank Piper was the headteacher and I was taught by Mr Yates (geography), Mr Gledhill (French), Miss Gradwell (English), Mrs Staines (maths), Mr

Staff at High Green Secondary Modern School in 1960. Frank Piper, headmaster, is seated in the middle of the front row.

Fullelove (music) and Mrs Jones (PE). I was never sport-minded but loved the arts and always sang in the choir, taking part in events such as Ecclesfield Music Festival and the school carol services which were always held in Mount Pleasant chapel. I still have the bible which was given to me on entry to the school and as tradition dictated on the last day of my school life I had staff and friends sign the inside cover as a memento.

I was lucky enough to be chosen to be head girl of the school and again still have my badges (green for the choir and blue to denote my house – Wentworth). The houses were Wentworth (blue), Wharncliffe (green), Whitley (red) and Wortley (yellow). For each assembly the captains and vice captains of each team and the head boy and head girl stood in front of the hall.

Janet Haddock (née Womersley), born 1946

School Trips

I remember taking our pupils on a school trip to Windsor. Coming back in the tube I sat opposite a lady who had a label on her lapel which said, 'Royal Enclosure, Ascot.' I, too, had a label on my lapel, it said, 'High Green Secondary Modern School'!

We used to collect excursion money on Monday mornings. One morning a pupil brought her contribution for the 'exertion'! We always called it the exertion after that.

Joan Gradwell

Setting off for a school camp from High Green Secondary Modern School, 1950.

CHAPTER 4

The War Years

Members of the local Civil Defence unit march down Wortley Road, High Green, during the Second World War.

Blitz

When the war came in 1939, every home was given an Anderson shelter to keep us safe from air raids, and as my father was not keen on gardening he welcomed putting it up, as it was less digging for him to do. My father was in the AFS, the volunteer fire service, and when the sirens went he put his uniform on and we didn't see him until about half an hour after the all clear had sounded. His station was the ARP post on Station Road, opposite Green's Foundry. On the Sunday night raid on Sheffield in December 1940, some incendiary bombs were dropped near Strawberry Avenue where I lived. Mr Allen, who lived on our road, had some stables and a smallholding on Blind Lane (now called Colley Road) from where he ran a firelighter and stick business. When the incendiary bombs dropped, his place caught fire, and my dad was called to put it out.

I went to school on the Monday following the Sunday night raid and only seven of us turned up. Going over Tunwell and down 'the hollow' and 'the gulley' towards school we picked up shell nose cones and shrapnel from the guns which were stationed on the Hunshelf. This started a display in school as we all took in what we had found.

Lewis Burrows, born 1927

Sheltering From Bombs

On Thursday 11 December 1940, when the Germans bombed Sheffield, we were in our Anderson shelter at Hesley Bar and my mother looked out. She thought our bungalow was burning but it was the field, all lit up with incendiary bombs. I was in my siren suit and shrapnel came down thick and fast. A bomb was dropped on Warren – we went to see the crater the next day. Later on I used to visit the Dutch evacuees at Bracken Hill Camp and take them for walks. I once made a toy for them, it was a golliwog, and it was much admired by the children.

Elvy Ibbotson (née Layte), born 1928

Wartime at High Green House

The war added surprises, extra vividness, as well as two evacuees: Mary and Alan. My brothers, father and grandfather appeared in uniforms (John, Indian Army; Syd, Navy; father, Special Constable; grandpa, Home Guard); shrapnel came through the roof, the kitchen ceiling was brought down; we used the large pantry with its stone-slab harbouring buckets of eggs in waterglass, as an air-raid shelter and I was anxious because the dog had no gas mask. We children were too young to grasp the real worries of this time: running, after raids, to find 'souvenirs' and I later discovered, awful irony, incendiary cases in the toy cupboard! The air-raid practices at Junior School were exciting – singing in the shelter's long tunnels lit by paraffin lamps, which cast ghoulish shadows. My gas mask was jostled in its box by a series of treasures: conkers, whipping top, lead-thrower for hop-scotch, chalk...War meant clogs instead of wellingtons, cosseting gas mantles (candles or torches used for going to bed), and stone hot-water bottles (which crashed out of bed in the small hours). Mrs Hoggard made overnight cake from few ingredients, we tried dried bananas – brown and sticky – and always had junket with our summer fruits. My sweet 'points' never lasted beyond a week, usually jettisoned on blended-chocolate hard enough to crack teeth.

One Christmas Day we had three men from the Army camp join us. I've never forgotten the water-diviner pacing round our drawing room with a large twig twisting down from his hands. I longed to have 'the gift' but none of us had. Later, white Americans arrived at the camp and small boys began running up Potter Hill with fish and chips for them, chewing gum as the reward. Black Americans came next whom we viewed with amazement, then POWs, Italians who filled our cinema and were given little bags of toffee by the cashier. They seemed to have more freedom than the German POWs, although I recall a

Members of the Harrison family of High Green House in uniform. Left to right: John Harrison, Indian Army; A.C. Harrison, Special Constable; Grandpa Hodgkins, Home Guard; and Syd Harrison, Royal Navy.

blond German diving superbly at Howbrook Reservoir.

Janet Harrison, born 1932

Wartime Work

In 1942 when I was nearly seventeen years old I started work at Newton Chambers core-making for the moulders and then I was testing incendiary bombs and stamping them with a special mark if they were all right. A government official worked alongside me and stamped them with a government mark if they were ready for use. About a year later I had the chance to work on the overhead cranes, something I really wanted to do. The crane was reached by climbing a near-vertical metal ladder. The work involved manoeuvring the controls in order to lift and transport heavy ladles of molten metal. It required precision and concentration, as the moulders would shout instructions to me in the noisy bay, telling me to lift or lower the ladle. On the day shift we usually started work at 7.30 a.m. until 5 p.m. Sometimes we had to work for twelve hours. On the alternate week we worked nights – 7.30 p.m. until 7.30 a.m.

During the blackout I used to walk from Charlton Brook to Thorncliffe with Denis Myers and Sam Williams. We sometimes used to bump into Italian prisoners-of-war from the camp and black Americans too when they were stationed at the camp. We had one night off each week. If the sirens went you had to come down a weighted rope mechanism, the difficulty was remembering exactly where you were

Thelma Dransfield (later Gregory), crane driver at Newton Chambers in the Second World War.

because the electricity went off immediately. Two cranes operated in each bay and there were six bays – four for heavy castings, one for fettling and one for light castings. We were making castings for Churchill tanks and for ships. I worked with George Sheldon, Jack Parry, Claud Perry and Jack Hawksworth. We knew everybody. The bay where my brother, Horace, worked I knew them as well – the Deardens, Jack Knight, Eric Smith from Grenoside, Harvey Kay, they were all local lads. During the war all the crane drivers were girls but when the men started coming back from the war we had to come out of the cranes and the men took over. I loved my work and was sad to leave. I then moved into the laboratories, testing moulding sand, but I was on my own most of the time and didn't enjoy that work as much.

Thelma Gregory (née Dransfield), born 1925

Sewing Bees

We had 'sewing bees' and I can remember Miss Kelly (one of our teachers at St Mary's Roman Catholic School) coming to our house to sew. We 'borrowed' a couple of my dad's flat caps and took the brims off and neatened them up for sailor hats, they were quite the fashion sailor's hats! Our Mary laughs to this day about a cardigan she knitted me, it was simply scarves unravelled, and, of course, striped!

Margaret O'Toole (née Rice), born 1930

The Jawbone Searchlight

In the early 1940s the War Department decided to ring Sheffield with a girdle of searchlights, barrage balloons, anti-aircraft guns and Observer Corps units, all of which were to be sited on the crests of the surrounding hills. One such position for a searchlight was the corner of a pasture field just across the road from the Birley Stone, Grenoside, and so Lane Head found itself on the frontline of Sheffield's air defences. The decision having been made, two circular, sand-bagged pits were excavated – one for the searchlight and the other for a mounted Lewis gun.

The next decision was that of finding accommodation for the subaltern and his platoon who were to operate this arrangement. The nearest property of any size was Lane Head House with its range of outbuildings and a semi-derelict one-up and one-down cottage. This cottage was upgraded with reinforced concrete, given a new floor and staircase and the whole then protected with blast walls – to all intents and purposes it resembled a battle headquarters – such was the accommodation for the lieutenant and his batman. The platoon, on the other hand, was instructed to fill their palliasses with our stock's bedding straw and to make their quarters in the stone barn above the cow standing and stables where at least they would be warm. We had concerns about this arrangement as the men were inclined to smoke NAAFI fags whilst reclining on the straw, which was adjacent to the Dutch barn which was stacked to the roof with the winter supply of hay. The situation was resolved without the knowledge of the top brass by Lieutenant Jarvis moving in with our family and his platoon bedding down in the cottage.

The searchlight required a reliable source of electric current which could not be supplied by the YEB so a mobile generator was positioned in the corner of the field at Lane Head crossroads and a cable was run out to the hill top position. As soon as this generator started up we knew to expect an air raid some ten minutes later – for us the Civil Defence siren was unnecessary. We would then retreat to the arched, stone-roofed subterranean dairy at the back of the house, light the paraffin lamp and heater and hope for the best. Whenever there was a non too distant explosion the flames would dip and rise again. The nearest delayed action bomb came to rest in Wheata Wood near the top end of Rough Lane. The large crater might still be extant to this day. For us children the evidence was exciting and I well remember seeing a magpie pinned to an adjacent tree by a piece of shrapnel. My father who had experienced trench warfare seemed to take it all in his stride and confidence rose to such a level that we would shelter under the large stone gateposts to watch the 'show' over Sheffield and the sparks raised by the anti-aircraft shrapnel striking the road surface. Nose cones were particularly prized.

It was not uncommon for the searchlight to develop a 'fault' at a time when it should have been activated. In truth, the young soldiers were terrified in case some German aircraft gunner should loose a few rounds down the beam. Very often too the Lewis gun, which was in fact very poor protection, was out of action either through age or the gunner not being au fait with the mechanism. It was not unknown for my father (as a civilian) to be smuggled onto the site to sort out a fault from what he could remember about the weapon from 1917. On other days it was not uncommon to see a line of soldiers crawling across the corner of the field searching for the firing pins in the long grass.

As the war progressed I was excused sleeping in the dairy and instead given unofficial permission to sleep amongst the equipment racks in the adjacent bomb-proof cottage amid the carbon rods for the light, the ammunition, and the tempting imported fruit. When the unit dispersed the bomb-proof cottage reverted to sheltering broody hens sitting on goose eggs – had we later to have had an atomic war these hens would have been the only survivors of Grenoside!

George Robinson

Doris Smith (later Fox) in her Land Army uniform.

Women's Land Army

I was in the Women's Land Army for almost five years during the Second World War. My first placement was at Bingham's Farm in Townend Road, Ecclesfield where I stayed for about a year. First thing in the morning, about six o'clock, I had to milk the cows by hand, no machines in those days, then feed and muck out all the animals. Then I got changed and went with Mr Bingham on the milk round. We delivered milk all round Shiregreen and he taught me to drive the car which had an open back to carry the milk churns – no milk bottles then. People used to leave a basin on the window sill and I used to measure out a pint or two from a two gallon milk churn. When we got back we had lunch and then I went to work in the fields, sowing or reaping depending on the season. Turnips, potatoes, sprouts and cabbages were all grown and when they were ready I had to cut, weigh and bag them. In June it was hay time and in September it was harvest time. About teatime Mr Bingham would say, 'You knock off Doris, round up the cows (there was no dog, only me) and start milking and we'll join you when we've finished here.' Sometimes I'd nearly finished the milking by the time they came. There were about thirty cows. Afterwards I had to wash the equipment in the dairy, put the milk into the churns and then it was time for our evening meal about six o'clock.

After about a year I decided to ask for a transfer to be near my brother, a policeman, in Leeds and I was sent to Quarry House Farm at Askwith, near Otley. It was very isolated and I got one day off a fortnight, a Sunday, and even then I had to milk the cows at 6 a.m. before my free time. Unfortunately there was no transport on Sundays but I managed to get a lift into Leeds on the Milk Marketing Board lorry which was collecting the milk churns from farms. I stayed at that farm for almost a year.

In 1942 I moved to Easingwold where a number of Land Girls stayed in a YWCA hostel under the direction of a warden called Mrs Grace. Farmers would ring up and ask for a number of girls depending on the job. We were all issued with a bike and we worked from eight in the morning until five in the evening. While I was there it was the ninetieth anniversary of the YWCA and there was a national celebration and fund-raising. I was chosen to present a purse containing £90 to Princess Elizabeth (later to become our Queen) at the Albert Hall in London. The money had been raised by the Land Girls in the Terrington, Stockton and Easingwold hostels. I was terribly nervous and travelled to London on the Friday ready for the ceremony on the Saturday. I had been booked into the Baker Street YWCA but when I got there discovered that it had been overbooked. There were Land Girls from all parts of the country and they put us in an underground subway. I never got a wink of sleep all night – the girls were chatting, singing and telling jokes. I was so tired and worried in case I made a mistake. My mum and Auntie Ada had travelled down to watch. I took my place on stage at the Albert Hall. You had to curtsey, shake hands and hand the purse to Princess Elizabeth who shook hands and said thank you. I felt really honoured.

I was based at Easingwold for three years before being released from Land Army duties. It was jolly hard work and little pay, but we had the satisfaction of 'doing our bit' for the war effort by replacing the young farmers who had gone to war.

Doris Fox (née Smith), born 1920

Rationing

Food was rationed during the war. Everyone was issued with a ration book which contained pages of small coupons. The rations were very small. At one time I know we had only 25gm of butter per week each and 12gm of cheese – hardly a mouthful. Families had to register with shops for rationed goods. My mother registered with the Meadow Dairy for butter, cheese and eggs and with the Co-op for meat, sugar and tea, the theory being that you stood a better chance of getting extras if you were registered in two shops. Occasionally the woman in the Meadow Dairy would slip me a jar of pineapple jam, which was really made from turnips with pineapple flavouring.

My favourite meal was dried egg omelette. Although fresh eggs were rationed we were able to buy tins of dried egg which was mixed with water to use in cooking. I liked the taste and it was very filling. Sweets were rationed so we looked for alternatives like liquorice root, which was much healthier and lasted a long time.

Aileen Thompson (née Bagshaw), born 1933

The Kelly Lamp

When my mother had to go into a nursing home because of failing health, and we began to clear her home of all her belongings, in a box of things in the outhouse I came across an item which I had not seen since the war years and which brought back memories of those times – a small Kelly lamp.

Many who lived through those years will remember these lamps. The 'Kelly' was a small paraffin lamp, and ours had a green enamelled base about three inches in diameter, bowl-shaped and slightly flattened at the bottom, which was weighted. It would normally stand upright, but if accidentally knocked over, it would safely right itself like a 'Kelly' doll. Above the sealed-in weight was the fuel reservoir holding about a cupful of paraffin, and screwed into this was the wick holder. Made of brass, the upper part of this ring of 'fingers', which lightly but firmly held the translucent white glass shade, always reminded me of a king's crown.

I remember it first being used during the air-raids of 1940, when I was four years old and everything seemed a big adventure. During an air-raid warning, a blackout of household lights was required, but dad, in any case, turned the gas off at the meter for safety, and the Kelly lamp became our portable light source, much safer and brighter than a candle.

When the raids first started, we tried using the shelters which had been purpose-built at the bottom of Westbrook Road, taking Kelly with us because we never knew what light would be available. However, we found that most of the shelters had been 'bagged' by those living nearest.

It was decided that we should be better off staying at home, since, apart from these frustrations, if we happened to be in transit to the shelters when the Hunshelf Ack-Ack Battery started firing at approaching German bombers, we were likely to be showered with shrapnel from their shells. The acknowledged 'safest' place in our houses was the pantry under the stairs, and this was duly re-organized as our shelter, with three old beer crates acquired to sit

American soldiers march down Wortley Road at High Green.

on, and the Kelly lamp on a high shelf of its own, shedding its comforting light on us as we huddled together, listening to the drone of the bombers and the thud of the guns, and waiting for the 'all clear' siren to sound.

Ted Bellamy, born 1936

The Yanks are Coming!

During the Second World War when I was about nine years old I was on Market Street in Chapeltown when the first American soldiers arrived. They wanted some fish and chips from Platts' fish and chip shop but during the war you had to take your own newspaper for wrapping them in and, of course, they didn't have any with them. I said I could get some and went chasing into our house on Smith Street for a *Daily Herald* or two. They were so pleased that they folded a sheet of the newspaper and passed it round the truck and the soldiers filled it with boiled sweets, candies, chewing gum (the sort in long flat strips not the kind we knew in tablet form) and some cigarettes, Lucky Strike and Camel for my dad. I was delighted with the sweets and astonished as it was the first time I had seen a black man. I took my treasure home where my brother, Keith, was in bed, poorly with asthma. He was upstairs in the front bedroom. We'd never seen as many sweets for ages. We had those sweets for a fortnight before we ate one! We used to count them and share them out about four times a day!

Derek Renshaw, born 1934

A Welcome For All

High Green Working Men's Club had a liberal, democratic and co-operative attitude no better reflected than the way in which it welcomed soldiers from the nearby camps in the Second World War. High Green Camp (at Potter Hill) first had soldiers from the Nottingham area and I remember four young recruits in particular (quiet, non-drinkers) who found refuge and friendship at the club. Indeed my mother wrote to their families in reassurance and each grateful household returned her kindness by welcoming our family into their homes during our annual holiday. My mother provided cream cracker and cheese sandwiches from the bar (surely the cheese was contributed from miners' rations) and chocolate biscuits (provided, I think, by the committee) and even tea and coffee for non-drinkers. Later when the American soldiers were billeted at the local camps and the public houses decided to designate themselves 'black' or 'white' pubs in order to avoid trouble, the club continued to welcome anyone in uniform. I remember one quiet, black American who missed playing the piano and so any evening he wanted to play he sat at our piano in the front room, his supper waiting on the top of the piano. Class was no barrier either. There was a wealthy, white American soldier, just qualified as a doctor who was encouraged by those sitting at the bar to give a demonstration of the 'jitterbug', as American jiving was called. I was called in by my sister to watch this. His energetic and enthusiastic performance was greatly enjoyed and loudly applauded. On the other hand, a poor, white American, who was nicknamed 'Beano' enthralled quite a gathering with photographs of himself as a boy in bread queues in the New York slums during the Depression. He hadn't known at the time that he was being photographed and had purchased the photographs much later when he recognised them in some publication. His accounts of his poverty-stricken childhood were fascinating and quite at variance with the idea of American life we were assuming from the cinema at the time.

The pianist, the jiver and 'Beano' each wrote to my mother after the war thanking my parents for their particular kindness and expressing gratitude for the comradeship the membership shared with them when they were away from home and preparing for active service.

Pat Cunningham (née Walton), born 1933

Germs and Germans

We were pretty healthy during the war in spite of the food shortages, or maybe because of them, though when anyone did become ill it was a serious matter. In 1940 or 1941 I caught scarlet fever. We were staying with my mother's sister, Meg, at Kirkby in Ashfield in Nottinghamshire. I don't remember feeling ill at first, but I do remember feeling very grumpy and irritable one day. During the night I became delirious and the doctor was sent for. He diagnosed scarlet fever which was very serious at that time. I was taken in an ambulance back to Sheffield – I can't remember that, I was too ill – and put into the fever ward at Lodge Moor Hospital, the other side of Sheffield from where we lived. There was another ward for diphtheria patients, a dreaded disease, as so many children who caught it died from it. I was there for about six weeks, and as I began to get better I was very bored. For most of the time I was the only patient in the fever ward, though the diphtheria ward was full. When the air-raid siren went at night we were all taken down into the basement and put together. I was far more frightened of catching diphtheria than I was of being bombed. I tried to hold my breath, so that I wouldn't breathe in diphtheria germs, and it obviously worked. Visitors were allowed one day a week for an hour, and because of the fear of infection, had to stand outside the building to shout through a closed window. My parents had a journey of about one and a half hours to get to the hospital, then stand in the cold shouting through a window to a weeping child. I found those visits very upsetting, and was only consoled when the nurses brought in the things that my family had brought me. I had never had so many presents. One in particular seemed wonderful. I was very fond of colouring and painting, and someone sent me a painting set shaped like an artist's palette. I wasn't allowed to paint at the hospital, of course, but looked forward to creating a masterpiece when I got home. Sadly, this wasn't to be, as everything had to be left at Lodge Moor, in case of infection! My Auntie Meg never forgave me for getting scarlet fever at her house – it had to be fumigated by the authorities. For years afterwards she reminded me of it.

Aileen Thompson (née Bagshaw), born 1933

Wartime Help

A Land Army girl came to Rainstorth Farm during the Second World War called Marjorie Callis. Many years later we heard that she'd been killed by a grizzly bear in Canada. On threshing day we once had a team of German prisoners-of-war from Potter Hill Camp, under guard, of course. They were German officers and very educated. On the second day one of them gave my uncle a letter that he'd written asking for further days' work so that they wouldn't get transferred from Potter Hill. My uncle found them some work – they were muck leading, turnip cutting and all sorts. They were real workers. They didn't go in the house for anything, they had a mug of cocoa and their sandwiches in the stackyard.

There was always casual labour at haytime and harvest. Walt Grange used to come after work. He worked at Parker's File Works and finished at four o'clock. My aunt gave him his tea and then he would walk up to the field and take his singlet and shirt off and hang them on a tree to dry while he got on with things. There was also Mrs Oliver, Ollie, we called her. She was rather eccentric, poor as a church mouse and as honest as the day is long. When it was our birthday she would open her purse and give us sixpence even though she couldn't afford it. She used to do everything even haymaking and loading. Once after helping to load the dray and rope it up she came down the last rope. Stanley Waller, one of our workers, on seeing a woman coming down the rope said, 'Eyes down!' One lovely summer's day she came up the yard in a pair of their Jack's wellingtons. My uncle said 'they're four sizes too big for her, I bet she teks three bloody steps afore t' wellington shifts!'

John Greaves, born 1935

The following extracts are from the notebook of Special Constable George Arthur Marshall, Section Leader C167, written during 1943:

Special Constable Duties

Saturday 6 March 1943:
At 10.50 p.m. I was in bed at my home, when I was aroused by someone knocking at my door, I got up, and upon going to the door saw that there were several people outside including women. I was told that there was a man lying on the footpath at the opposite side of the road having a fit, I was also asked if I could do anything for him. I got some clothes on and went outside to the man, I spoke to him but got no reply. Upon examining him further, I found that he was dead drunk. His skin was cold and he had neither hat nor coat on, so I decided to take him into my house, as I did not know what serious consequences may develop from him lying on the cold footpath. With the help of two men I got him into my house, but owing to his drunken state we had to carry him. On the way he recovered a little and commenced to make use of bad language such as 'I'm bloody frozen' and other similar expressions. On getting him into the house, I laid him on the hearthrug in front of the fire, where it was warm, he then commenced to vomit all over the rug, down the side of the chair and over the fireplace...PC Paley was sent for and said that he would be reported for being drunk and incapable and to which he replied, 'It won't be t' bloody first time'.

Tuesday 13 April 1943:
In Penistone Road, Burncross, a driver from Millhouses was reported for using his car for pleasure (he was taking 'a woman to a public house') instead of business. On being told, the man said, 'I admit I'm wrong, definitely

Special constables from Burncross and Chapeltown, 1942-45. George Arthur Marshall is immediately left of centre in the second row.

Fancy dress parade outside the Queen's Head, High Green on VE Day.

wrong, but isn't there a way out, I shall lose everything?'

Tuesday 10 August 1943:
11.35 p.m. Warned the manageress Block 2 Bracken Hill Emergency Hostel Site of the serious consequences which would result from any further carelessness with regard to showing lights after blackout.

Sunday 28 November 1943:
9.00 p.m. On Duty. Watching for blackout thief in Chapel Row, Burncross.

Friday 31 December 1943:
A soldier in uniform was trying to sell for ten shillings 'two pairs of new whitish-grey men's pants'. They were Army issue. He was reported to Ecclesfield Police Station but 'while in the act of doing so, he slipped through a side door through the Barnes Hall farm yard and vanished from view'.

George Arthur Marshall

Doodlebug

In 1944 when I was seventeen years old the air-raid siren went one evening and my mother, two sisters and myself went in the shelter. For some reason that night my dad was not on duty with the fire service and he stayed in the house. I remember the gun fire, then all was quiet, so I went to my dad in the house to make a hot drink for the others.

The candlelight procession in Chapeltown Park, part of the victory celebrations, 1945.

While we were in the house we heard a noise coming from the street, so my dad opened the front door. He told me to put out the candle that he had lit and he went out. There was our next door neighbour and a few more men looking up into the sky, and talking about this thing flying, in a westerly direction, which I later learned was a Doodlebug or Flying Bomb.

These things were not supposed to have the range of flight to come inland as far as this, and I was really excited, yet frightened, as the engine noise was very strange and different from an aeroplane engine. It had a flame coming from the tail about four feet long and was going pretty fast. It appeared to have come over Chapeltown or Thorpe and flew across the sky the full length of Strawberry Avenue. I later learned that it had dropped near Hyde in the Manchester area.

Lewis Burrows, born 1927

VE Day

I shall never forget the end of the war in Europe. VE Day was 8th May 1945, the day before my twelfth birthday, but the celebrations in Chapeltown were on 9th May, my birthday. The whole day was like a huge birthday party for me, I don't think I ever felt so excited, a feeling shared by everyone else. Every child was given a torch – a thick cardboard handle with a huge candle in the end of it – and the whole village turned out to parade through the streets led by a brass band in which my father played the tuba. The parade ended in Chapeltown Park, with the band on the bandstand. Crowds of people ate, danced and sang until late at night by the light of the torches. I kept the remains of my torch for years as a reminder of that wonderful day.

Aileen Thompson (née Bagshaw), born 1933

CHAPTER 5

All in a Day's Work

Molten metal is teemed into a mould in the heavy castings foundry at Newton Chambers.

Horseman and Carter

In 1909, at the age of nine, I used to walk from Grenoside to Bradfield where my sister was in service to collect two shillings of her wage to help the family budget. One day, when I was returning from this errand, going up Stephen Lane, Mrs Ernest Thorpe called me and asked if I would like to work for her, weighing coal, which she sold by the half and the hundredweight. The wages were to be sixpence a week. I accepted the job but told her that I would not be able to go at dinner time as I had to take dinners to two men at Fox Hill quarry (for twopence a week). She said that was all right, I could go before school in the morning and in the evening and a full day on Saturday.

Sometimes I had to deliver coal to people who could not collect it themselves. I had customers at Wood End, Skew Hill, Topside, and other places and pushing a hundredweight of coal is no mean task. Sometimes the customers would give me twopence for taking the coal, sometimes just grumble. Mr Ernest Thorpe was the carter for Grenoside. He owned six horses and had carts and drays. He carted all manner of things – files, coal, etc. His horseman was a grand chap named John Hobson who was very kind to me. Before long I started to drive a horse and cart and fetch coal from Smithy Wood Pit. John Hobson used to tell me where he had delivered a load of coal so that I could go, along with one of my brothers to get the coal into the coal place for them. Sometimes he delivered a load of coke to the church and I would go with a barrow and wheel the coke around the church to the boiler house for fourpence. The headmaster, Mr Tom Fulleylove, who was also the church choirmaster, would allow me to go from school at 3.30 p.m. in the winter to get the coke moved before dark. I would then go to Thorpe's, fill up the barrows or help John to bed the horses down and feed them.

Sometimes I would take four horses at a time, riding one and the others on halters, up to St Helena to the fields belonging to Tom May, where they would graze until morning. Then, with a bowl of corn I would coax them to the gate, slip three halters on, climb the gate, and after opening it, mount on to one horse's back and ride down to the stables for about 7 a.m. John would have tidied round and got their feed in the manger. We would then comb and brush them down; John believed in well-groomed horses.

On one occasion, Turpin, a big Shire crossed horse had a nasty gash on his leg where he had been kicked by another horse when we went to collect him from St Helena fields. The vet came and stitched it and said it must be rested for a while. Later he said we should exercise him by letting him graze on the roadside down by the church. Before I went to school I took him down the road to graze. He enjoyed the grass which at that time, before motor cars, was sweet and clean and in the summer collected for winter feed. One morning he was quietly grazing when Sam Fairest's motor taxi – I think it was the first car to come to Grenoside – came rattling up. Turpin, being fresh with not working, kicked up his heels and kicked me over the field wall, but he didn't run away and settled after the noise had gone. I climbed painfully back over the wall, got hold of his halter and led him back to the stable. I then went to school saying nothing to anyone. Someone must have seen the incident, for about 9.30 a.m. Mr Thorpe and the headmaster came to our class and called me out of my place. They took me into the cloakroom, gave me an examination and decided I should go home. Mr Thorpe took me home and told my mother I was to stay at home for a day or two. It was not long before I was back on the job.

Wintertime was a tough time for carters at Grenoside. No matter where you went it was either uphill or down, and the roads were bad enough without ice and snow. When conditions prevailed Mr Thorpe would still somehow manage to get to Sheffield with his horse and dray, but getting back up to Grenoside was another thing. If he expected difficulties he would leave word with his wife to ask me to meet him, usually about 6 p.m. at Wadsley Bridge, with an extra horse, to help pull the load up Penistone Road or the Old Road as we called it in those days. I would gear up old

Prince, my favourite horse, in the lamp-lit stables, then with a paraffin lamp on the harness and dressed in a thick, warm coat I would get on Prince's back and set off in the dark and the snow to ride to Wadsley Bridge. When I got there, Mr Thorpe would be waiting and we would hitch Prince in front of Major and get under the tarpaulin dray cover and make our way up the Old Road. There was no necessity to drive, the horses knew their way back to the stables.

Arthur Andrews, born 1900

Working in a File Works

I left school at fourteen years old and got a job at David Parker's Excelsior File Works on Station Road, Ecclesfield. I enjoyed every minute of it. We all knew each other and worked well together. My first job in the morning was to clean the offices, then go to the top shop to start filing the files which had arrived from the makers, ready for them to be placed on the cutting machines. If anyone was absent from work, I would do their job – working on the emery wheels or the grinding wheels. On Friday afternoons, around three o'clock, I would start to sweep the floor of the main shop. Most people finished early to go to pay their clubs and such. I remember one Friday very well, in fact I shall never forget it. I had finished all the sweeping and cleaning except for one machine, which Jess Higgins was still using. I ran a Chocolate Club for my brother, Maurice, who was crippled because of an accident at Thorpe Hesley Pit. Everyone at Parker's knew Maurice, so most of them joined the club. They would pass the money to me each Friday when they had been paid. I went to Jess for her money. Hers was a very large machine called a Shardlow and it had a large 'worm' running alongside it. Jess told me to get the club card out of the box at the side of her machine. While I was bending over the machine she started it up and my hair became tangled in the worm. I was calling to her to stop but at first she didn't hear me. By the time she realised what was happening, all of my hair was caught. Well, panic stations then! Mr Hobson, one of the main men at Parker's, was sent for. When he came, he carried on alarming with Jess and then he set about completely dismantling the machine. I was trapped for around two hours while he worked, and everyone kept asking me if I was all right. I was a sight for sore eyes when I was freed, I can tell you, my hair was jet black with grease. I never thought it would come out but mum washed it three times in paraffin, and out came all the grease. Mr Hobson said how lucky I had been – one more turn of the worm and my scalp would have gone. I never went near Jess's machine again.

Kate Hoyland (née Fisher), born 1910

Pit Work

By the beginning of the 1914 war, industry in Grenoside was starting to decay. File cutting was being taken over as was spring knife and steel making. Even rug weaving was feeling the pinch. Young men were finding it harder to get work until recruitment came and 'Kitchener needs you' was the cry. Grenoside youths were willing to go. Miners were kept back to ensure production of coal. I left the brickworks and went to work at Wharncliffe Silkstone Pit with my brother.

I started at Wharncliffe Silkstone as a

This postcard depicts the victims of the explosion at Wharncliffe Silkstone Colliery on 30 May 1914.

pony driver when I was about fourteen years old, walking from Grenoside, for 1s 2d a day. We had to be at the pit no later than 5.50 a.m. in time to take out our check and lamp or you were not allowed to start that day. We had some hurried journeys. We had to stop many a time for a double 'un, a double shift – that was from ten minutes to six in the morning until ten o'clock at night. That was mining in those days!

I was working at Wharncliffe Silkstone at the same time as the explosion in 1914 when eleven men and boys lost their lives. It was our face that blew up. We were working in water at the time so it was a short shift – that meant we only worked five hours, rather that eight – because we were wet through. The water was pouring down on us all the time. On the day of the explosion we came out at eleven o'clock and I walked home as usual, wet through – there were no baths. I decided to go to the cinema and walked to Hillsborough to the pictures, it was only 3d. When I was coming back I met Ann Fleetwood and Harry Foster and my brother and he said, 'You're a lucky 'un, aren't you?' and I said 'Why, what's up?' and he said, 'Your seam's blown up, Baileys and them were killed.' Eleven were killed and four injured. The Baileys were on the cutting machine. They said that the machine was red hot and gases got to it and you see, in those days, anything would do as long as you were cutting and getting some work out.

Arthur Andrews, born 1900

Against the Odds

I started work as an office boy at Newton Chambers in the Colliery Transport Manager's office at Warren Bridge. We office boys were fascinated with the internal locomotives that travelled round the ironworks, the collieries and the coke ovens and we were occasionally given a ride. On 6 December 1917 one particular locomotive, called *Mortomley*, was pushing a run of wagons up a slope to the Coke Ovens. I was on an errand with a message. I ran and tried to jump on the locomotive but my foot slipped off the footplate under the wheels. The accident happened about three o'clock and caused a bit of a stir in the district. I was taken to the Sheffield Infirmary in a horse-drawn ambulance, arriving after five o'clock. By the time I got to the infirmary I was in need of blood transfusions. They had to take my foot off by the ankle, but they didn't do a very good job and the leg turned septic, so they had to amputate six inches below the knee. In 1917, of course, the war was on and a full train of wounded soldiers from France came once a week to the infirmary which had a special section for them. At Christmas I went into the next ward with the soldiers for a concert but I was too ill and they took me back to my own ward.

Arthur Andrews in his prime.

After six weeks they sent me home, but still with a septic leg, and I was in terrible pain. My parents sent for Dr Howard Sands who lived in Greenhead House with a surgery in the drive. He was the surgeon in charge of Wharncliffe War Hospital at the time. He confirmed that the leg was still septic and said that I ought to go back into hospital. But I was in such a state and said, 'I can't go back!' My parents and my aunt and uncle, who kept the Prince of Wales Inn, said, 'Couldn't you do it, doctor?' He must have agreed and arrangements were made for the operation to take place within a day or so. The bedroom was cleared (where the family went I haven't a clue) and the operation took place. Dr Barraclough was the anaesthetist and the lady next door, Mrs Copley, held my leg for Dr Sands to open up and clean. He bandaged it tightly for four or five days. The bed was then turned to the window and I had to bare my leg to the light and air. My father said it would never heal but in a matter of days it was obvious that the healing process was beginning. I was soon able to get out of bed and move around on crutches. I was on crutches for about eighteen months. Then I went to Ellis, Son and Paramore's of Spring Street in Sheffield to be fitted and supplied with an artificial leg. There was nothing sophisticated in those days.

Once I got used to my limb I went back to work. I was put to work as a clerk in the Time Office. I worked there for about a year but I wasn't very happy. I then went to the Furnace Hill office to train as a draughtsman and settled down fairly quickly. I went to evening classes at Lound School for three years and then did four years as an evening student in the Applied Science Department of Sheffield University. In my fourth year I was attending four nights a week. By this time we were living on South Road at High Green so my journey involved a walk to Chapeltown Railway Station and then a walk from the Midland Station in Sheffield to St George's Square where the Applied Science Department at the University was – all after a day's work. Unfortunately there were times when I had to stay at home because of a sore leg due to excessive walking. Eventually I became a draughtsman working many years for Mr D.A. Gilham, the Chief Engineer of the Collieries.

Elijah Dransfield, born 1904

Scraping a Living

In the 1920s and 1930s there were a large number of iron moulders in the area. Some worked at Newton Chambers, others at William Green's foundry, Robinson Royds (which later became Brightside Foundry), Parramore's, Greenside and Charlton Brook foundries. Iron castings weighed anything from a few ounces to several hundred tons. I made the gulleys in Concord Cemetery.

There was also a great deal of unemployment and there was real poverty. Many villagers tried to supplement their income by various means. All the farms in the 1920s grew potatoes and at harvest time the crop was ploughed out and the potatoes hand-picked and put into buckets and then emptied into hessian sacks. One farmer called Helliwell at Butterthwaite let it be known that pickers should assemble with a bucket on a certain day at 8.30 a.m. About thirty men, women and children gathered in his yard and he had to climb on a cart, select about a dozen and send the rest home.

Joseph Knott, born 1915

Toil and Trouble

At the age of fourteen I left school on a Friday and started work on the following Monday at the Thorncliffe Drift Colliery. I was taken in hand by an ageing deputy called William Sheldon. He introduced me to the ins and outs of conveying tubs of coal from the coal face to the pit surface where it was screened, washed and loaded for sale. After a few weeks I was transferred to the Barley Hall end of the colliery. The workings were reached via a shaft which was over 100 yards deep. I was told by my deputy

Workers at Brightside Foundry, Ecclesfield.

Mining for coal in Hesley Wood during the 1926 strike.

to take out a pit pony. I went to the stables where twenty to thirty ponies were kept. The horse keeper showed me how to put on the pony's gears. I then asked him where I had to go. 'Tek 'owd o' pony's tail,' he said, 'he'll tek thee.' He was quite right – I followed the pony, whose name was Smuts, holding my oil lamp, with its tiny flame. These lamps burned 'colsolene' and the slightest jar would extinguish the light and leave you in total darkness. The darkness of a mine has to be experienced to be believed. About this time the 1926 strike intervened and we had a rough time. My older brothers opened up a small pit near Tankersley golf course and we extracted many bags of coal. Jack Furness carted our sacks of coal home by horse-drawn dray. We paid him with sacks of coal – we had no money.

Len Smith, born 1911

Erecting Aerial Ropeways

At the end of the 1920s Newton Chambers decided to build a bicable aerial ropeway to transport slack from Thorncliffe Colliery to the Washery and one to transport dirt from Thorncliffe Colliery and Washery to Westwood tip. In both cases they replaced transport by railway wagons and manual unloading. About the same time the company decided to close down the coke ovens at Thorncliffe and Rockingham Gas Works and build a more modern coke and chemical plant at Smithy Wood. I was involved in many ways with the undertaking to install ropeways connecting Rockingham, Thorncliffe and Smithy Wood. Ropeways Ltd sent their surveyor, Mr Kendall, to make the survey. I assisted him together with a youth, Philip Senior, and two labourers. It took two weeks. Drawings

Aerial ropeway between the Thorncliffe Works and Smithy Wood Colliery and coking plant passing over White Lane, Chapeltown.

were prepared by Ropeways Ltd giving a profile of the land and levels for trestles, etc. Bridges were needed over roads in places, as were loading stations and angle stations. When we received the working drawings we proceeded with the foundations, as Newton Chambers was responsible for the foundations. I was given the job of setting out and organising the construction of the concrete foundations for the trestles. Philip Senior assisted me. We worked with seven labourers. Jack Jeffries transported materials for us in his lorry to the various sites. The manufacture of the steel structures was placed with various firms including Newton Chambers Boiler Shop. Ropeways Ltd appointed a resident engineer for the erection of the various stations and trestles. The bridge with trestles on it over White Lane in Chapeltown was manufactured and erected by Naylor Bros of Golborne, Lancashire. The haulage rope for the Rockingham to Smithy Wood section was 8 miles long. There were 225 buckets capable of carrying 15 cwt each. Warren Hill was the angle point on the system and was used as a halfway area for rope changing and handling. It was decided that the carrying ropes between Warren Hill and Hesley Park and Warren Hill and Rockingham were too long to allow the correct tension to be applied, so divide stations were erected in Hesley Wood and Black Lane. The ropes were cut and anchored to 20 ton concrete blocks and spring gears fitted to allow the correct tension to be applied. The weight boxes at Hesley Park Angle Station were replaced with ground anchorage concrete blocks and spring tension gear.

In 1942 Mr Townsend became the chief engineer for service and maintenance and I moved into purchasing. After a while I became purchasing officer for headquarters. The next thing to happen was, because of the threat of nationalisation of the coal mines, a separate company was created called Newton Chambers Collieries Ltd. and I was appointed deputy purchasing manager. Prefab offices had been built at Skiers Spring and colliery staff were moved into them from Thorncliffe prior to vesting day, 1 January 1947. They were later moved to Worsbrough Hall.

In the late 1950s I became personal assistant to Ken Sutcliffe and I was back once again with engineers. The AGM didn't want me to retire in 1966, but my wife did. The last job I did was to supervise the removal of the aerial ropeways. George Martyn and myself had put in the foundations for the bridge over White Lane. When the ropeway was being dismantled and sold, Ken Sutcliffe said to me, 'Tha pur it in, tha can organise 'em to tek it aht' and I had to organise Marple and Gillott to take everything down. I watched it happen.

Elijah Dransfield, born 1904

Cod and Chips, Please!

After leaving school at fourteen (in 1925) I worked in my father's fish and chip shop on Thompson Hill, High Green. I used to prepare the fish and potatoes and serve at night while my dad fried. When I was twenty trade was very poor so I went into domestic service at Elland for 12s 6d a week. It wasn't a bad place but I was terribly homesick and lonely. Once a month I went home for the half day, getting home at 3 p.m. and leaving again at

8.15 p.m. When I was about twenty-three trade improved so I came home. We were very busy in the shop. When war broke out we managed to keep a good supply of fat, and, as most things were rationed, people queued for fish and chips. We had to work very quickly sometimes. Because the shop was next to a bus terminal, orders would come from outlying villages, such as Pilley. The errand boy would jump off the bus, order twenty or so 'fish and chips, wrapped' and expect them to be ready to return on the same bus when it turned round for the return journey.

When I was married in 1938 I kept on working in the shop. Each morning I used to bone about seven stones of fish a day while mum and dad did the potatoes. The fish came from Grimsby and as there were no fridges the fish had to be fetched daily from Westwood Station, about a mile or so from High Green. I used to take the drug, a box on four wheels, to meet the train. The porter would lift the box on for me and I would go back through the wood. Dad would meet me at the bottom of Westwood Hill and we pushed and pulled the seven stones of fish back home. In the afternoon the fish was cut into pieces. The shop was open from 7 p.m. until midnight every night and at lunchtimes on Fridays and Saturdays.

Doreen Smith (née Ashton), born 1911

Joe Ashton outside his fish and chip shop on Thompson Hill, High Green.

Wedding of Len Smith and Doreen Ashton, 1938.

Apprentice Stove Grate Fitter

I commenced my apprenticeship as a fitter in the stove and grate shop at William Green's works on Station Road when I left school at the age of fourteen. All young lads like myself wore clogs for work as indeed some of the men did. I slept in the front bedroom and could hear people going to work from as early as five o'clock in the morning as they tramped to work in their clogs. My mum made me a meat and potato pie in a small basin in winter which I took to work and got it warmed up for dinner. One icy morning my clogs were like skates and I took off on the ice. The basin broke and I had gravy all over my overalls all day.

Lewis Burrows, born 1927

Delivering Milk in Grenoside

Although I was born on the farm at Topside, I wasn't allowed to do much until I left school and then had to take the milk round with my father. In those days, we delivered milk twice a day in the village, taking the milk right into the customers' houses, measuring it out and pouring it into their own jugs – sometimes into 2lb jam jars (which just held one pint). We called them 'Parson Cross cream jugs'!

The milk was still warm and we carried it in gallon bottles made of stainless steel, along with a stainless steel measure. When the bottle was empty it was refilled from one of the large churns carried in the milk float. Any milk left over at the end of the day was put in the cellar in large pancheons, so the cream could rise to the top. The next day it

Mr and Mrs Frank Lowe deliver milk on Penistone Road, Grenoside in the early 1930s.

would be skimmed off with a special stainless steel plate with holes in it, to be sold or made into butter.

The old milk was then sold at half-price – 1½d per pint – which customers purchased from the farm. I remember once having to go round with the milk with a horse-drawn sledge because the snow was too deep for the cart wheels.

Marjorie Wilson (née Lowe)

General Maid at Mortomley Hall

When I went for my interview I was asked what my wages had been as kitchen maid at Barnes Hall. I said five shillings a week. I was told I would get six shillings a week but no-one to help me with the cooking and cleaning, only a woman on a Monday to do the washing – but not mine, I had to do that myself or take it to my mother. My routine was as follows:

I was up by 6 a.m. to make the fires in the kitchen, drawing room and study and on Mondays to clean the brass fireplace in the lounge after there had been a fire lit there on the Sunday. Then I had to clean the drawing room and take tea upstairs for Dr and Mrs Gault and their daughter and then have my own breakfast when I could.

While they were having breakfast I would go into the surgery and make sure all the chairs were dusted and that there were plenty of medicine bottles ready, and open the door at 8.30 a.m., ready for the patients to come in. Then I had to clean the study, wash the breakfast things, go upstairs and do the beds and vacuum and dust. By this time it was time to make coffee before the doctor went out on his rounds. Then I had to clean the kitchen and start getting lunch ready. I never knew what time the doctor would be back but Mrs Gault always said have it ready for dishing up.

After lunch and the washing up done, I had to tidy the drawing room again and then clean the surgery, fetch more medicine bottles and wash them ready for the evening surgery. Then I would change my uniform ready to take tea into the study. The surgery door was opened at four o'clock and then I got dinner ready which was eaten around eight o'clock after the doctor had finished for the day (he hoped). I would have my own dinner while I was waiting for him to finish surgery. After dinner and the washing up done I had to mop the surgery floor ready for next morning. Around 10 p.m. I would take the drinks tray into the study. Then I could sit down to a hot drink before going to bed. More often than not the door bell would ring in the night and I had to go down and answer it and get the doctor up. I then had to wait till he came back and have a hot drink ready for him.

I had one so-called half day a week. This started at 4 p.m. when I opened the surgery door and I had to be in by 9 p.m. and always had the dinner things to wash and the surgery to clean before I could go to bed. I was allowed to go home for one hour on Friday night to take my wage and I never once had a Sunday free.

Doreen Womersley (née Goddard), born 1925

Wedding of Herbert Womersley and Doreen Goddard in 1945.

Harvesting oats at Rainstorth Farm, Ecclesfield in the 1930s.

All I Ever Wanted To Do

My Uncle Roland moved onto Rainstorth Farm in 1929. It was a mixed farm then of eighty-four acres. He had eighteen dairy cows, milked by hand of course, some land was for summer grazing and some ploughed – geared to feeding the livestock. In addition to the cattle we had three working horses, shires. We grew succulents for the animals – turnips, kale and mangolds. Some fields were never ploughed because they were too poor and steep or a bit boggy and the rest was on a rotation, a four year ley and then they would be ploughed up into wheat and then perhaps oats and then turnips, mangolds, kale or potatoes and then back to spring corn and then undersown for another four years. The horses were given the best of everything.

My parents also lived on the farm, my father had a milk round and always had a few pigs and some poultry. He understood poultry, our front room was often full of incubators and chickens chirping. He used to send for pedigree cockerels, mostly from the south coast. He had Rhode Island Reds, Light Sussex and Brown Leghorns. Leghorns were the best layers but the others were more meaty. He delivered milk in Ecclesfield and Chapeltown but finished when he was called up for Army service in 1944. When my uncle died in 1957 my father bought the farm in my name.

When I was a little lad all I ever wanted to do was to go in the fields and work with the men and do what they were doing. I remember once, when I was about three, my uncle and his workmen came past the farmhouse after tea with their forks. They were cocking up in the Twelve Acre. The hay had been raked up in the afternoon into windrows and they were making it into hay-cocks. My uncle brought me a little broken fork and I went with them. They started off, my uncle leading and I tagged on the end thinking I was going to keep up with them. I started on this hay-cock and when I looked up they were three or four windrows away from me. I remember thinking I'm not doing very well here and I wanted to make a good 'un. I found out years later that I actually climbed on a hay-cock and fell asleep and they carried me home when they'd done. But it's nice to know now that whenever I go to the Twelve Acre I was there sixty-one years ago.

John Greaves, born 1935

Thorncliffe Apprentice

My dad obtained a position for me, subject to a successful interview, as an apprentice draughtsman at Thorncliffe. I started in August 1949, having successfully completed my School Certificate, with a wage of £1 a week. As instructed I reported to the pre-entry course schoolroom right at the centre of the works and was met by Mr Jack Dorgan, the training officer, and twenty-nine other young men who were about to begin their apprenticeships. Before the day was over we had been medically examined and issued with sets of dark blue boiler suits, listened to a series of lectures on the history of the company, its products, our training schemes, what was expected from us during our service, health and safety and a host of other things. The following four weeks were spent visiting the various workshops, listening to more in-depth lectures, doing physical education, doing physical work at the Scout Camp in Hesley Wood, tree-felling, clearing bracken, building fireplaces and tables, and being screened for our future employment. At the end of this I was appointed to be the office boy in the Recuperator drawing office, under the supervision of Mr Ken Sheard and Mr Ron Hallam, in the Heavy Castings Division of the Company.

I was allowed to do detail drawings of parts under the supervision of a draughtsman, and it was my job to take drawings and material lists to the pattern shop and the machine and fitting shops, as well as make tea and wash the draughtsmen's cups. Another job was to take the draughtsmen's drawings through to the tracing office, then under the supervision of Miss Archer, where eight or ten young ladies carefully and beautifully traced the draughtsmen's pencil drawings onto starched translucent linen sheets in Indian ink to make a long-lasting, permanent record of them. It was in this office, and at this time, that I met my future wife, Pat Rawson.

In September 1949 I commenced day release and one evening a week at Barnsley Mining and Technical College in Mechanical Engineering. Following the next intake of pre-entrants, I went to the Foundry Training School for four weeks' introduction to foundry work. Schoolroom instruction was given in metallurgy, moulding techniques, sands and binders, and moulding. Practical work was carried out in a small fenced off area where we were instructed in the art of sand casting, managing melting techniques and casting. I then spent six months as an assistant to a skilled pattern maker. During my workshop training I was selected as one of the apprentices to attend the service, in Sheffield Cathedral, at the Installation of Sir Harold West as Master Cutler in October 1952.

I returned to the Foundry School for a further month's training, this time to a new purpose-built school behind the White House Building, where a small cupola melting furnace had been provided. This was followed by six months in the Light Casting Foundry. Two periods were then spent in the Machine Shop School and twelve months in the machine shop.

I then entered the light castings drawing office, designing and drawing a variety of Redfyre products, the Redfyre 55 all night burning inset fire, modifications to the Redfyre combination cooking range, and the first of a series of slow combustion stoves. I also had to carry out tests to assess the radiant and convective efficiency of the products and prepare and undertake cooking tests on the cooking appliances, all as specified in the various British Standards applicable to the respective appliances.

Apprentices' dinner, Newton Chambers, 1952. Chris Morley is at the back on the left.

A representative group of Newton Chambers apprentices attending the Installation of Sir Harold West as Master Cutler at Sheffield Cathedral in 1952.

The apprenticeship training provided by Newton Chambers & Co. was superb. The teaching was thorough and clear, the practical work and training were equally good. The men we apprentices were allocated to were patient and understanding, and, of course, the social activities were many and varied. Dances, dinners, outings, interesting visits, and the many clubs and societies run by the Recreational Society were well patronised and enjoyable.

Chris Morley, born 1933

Apprentice at Hall and Pickles

I was one of the rogues who was an apprentice at Hall and Pickles in the small tool engineering department from 1954 to '60. We were taken on aged fifteen and were happy to stay there after the age of twenty-one, secure and with a steady job. Mr Murphy was the works manager and Fred Haslam was manager of the tool department.

We had a thorough grounding in good workshop practices such as machine maintenance – 'If t' notice says oil it weekly, then oil it lad!' We spent six months on each job – turning, milling, grinding and in the drawing office before settling on one section when we were eighteen years old. There was also day release to go to Rotherham Technical College to study for our City and Guilds.

However it wasn't all noses to the grindstone and I think we broke more sweat during the dinner hour than in the workshops. We did plenty of larking about – damming up the Blackburn Dyke, which

Apprentices and staff of Hall and Pickles, tool engineering department, 1956. David Crisp is on the back row, third from the right.

caused flooding, and pinging the pots on the telegraph poles with ball bearings shot from 'works-made' catapults.

Apprentices were fortunate at Hall and Pickles because, not only were we given a sound training but help was always on hand, whatever the problem. I was going to a Scout Jamboree at Lake Bala, Wales in 1957 and needed a bike. The maintenance department decided I should have one. Someone brought in a frame, others wheels, even panniers, all put together in the shop. It was a proud day when I set off for Bala riding my HYDRA, brightly painted in the firm's green and yellow colours.

Every apprentice had the chance to go for a month to an Outward Bound Centre with everything paid for including sandwiches for the journey. I went to Aberdovey where, never a sailor, I even managed to enjoy a three-day sail in a ketch to Ireland! It was a wonderful experience being an apprentice at Hall and Pickles. I remember the camaraderie and the satisfaction of learning to do a job well.

David Crisp, born 1940

A group of workers at Hall and Pickles.

CHAPTER 6

Leisure and Pleasure

Thompson Hill, High Green. High Green Picture Palace is the large building on the right.

Recreation at Grenoside

For recreation we had the maypole on May Day and sports and tea parties at Whitsuntide and Christmas. In the winter there were chapel socials, the Band of Hope night was a special night with games and recitations. The superintendent was Bill Senior, an elder of the chapel. The meetings were held in the old Primitive Methodist chapel where the only lighting was a ring of gas jets in the roof. These were lit by a lighted taper on the end of a long pole. This pole served another purpose; old Bill would sit in the pulpit watching the games being played by the children and if he thought you were getting a bit boisterous down would come the pole on your anatomy somewhere and you settled down. They must have been dedicated people to give their time to give us a bit of pleasure, and teach us religion. There were many good instrumentalists –

Walter Sharp, Bill Sharp, Miss Burkinshaw, Lily Sharp, Hector Ellison, Tom Fulleylove, Alice Gledhill, the Nuttalls, Farewell Hobson and his double bass which he and his son, Hugh, carried all over the circuit giving their assistance along with some good voices to other chapels. On one occasion one of the chapels was singing the *Messiah* and had borrowed a bass player. They were going nicely when the bass player complained that the light was too bad so they asked a boy to stand by the player's music stand with a lighted candle. When it came to the 'Crown Him' chorus the boy was a bit fed up and so was the player who was heard to say after each 'Crown Him', 'Howd bloody leet up'.

Christmas time was always a time of music and singing for weeks before Christmas. If you were passing Grenoside Working Men's Club and Institute you would hear melodious sounds of Christmas hymns, some of which were never heard elsewhere. It seemed to be a custom in the old days that each village had its own Christmas carols. As boys we would black our faces, carry a pick, a shovel or riddle and go around the village, including the pubs, singing *Six Jolly Miners*. Letting Christmas in was also the order of the day for Christmas morning. You would sing the shortened version of a carol, say the shortened version of a rhyme and listen. If you didn't get word you were too early or too late, you waited patiently for the door to open and a hand offering you a penny or twopence, if you were lucky. Having a coal round, as I had, proved useful at this time, I would call on all my customers and sing (I had a decent voice in those days) and was rarely denied a copper or two. Nearly every child in Grenoside would go down to visit Mr Bellhouse at Greno House. You had hardly opened your mouth to sing when Norah Cooper, the housekeeper, pushed a penny in your hand – 'Thank you, next please.'

Chapeltown and High Green Picture Palaces were very popular. At High Green the only sound was a piano, with Muriel, the pianist, trying hard to compete with the picture – horses galloping, cowboys singing, the *Charge of the Light Brigade* – and pellets of toffee paper being fired from a bit of garter elastic by the boys in the audience. Sometimes the music stopped and Muriel went on strike and then Mrs Woofenden chased the offenders from the Picture Palace with her stick.

The Machens of Skew Hill were a robust family, prepared to tackle any kind of sport. Joe Machen and Reden Machen were considered the champion knur and spell players of the world and prepared to meet all comers. Around the time of the First World War Grenoside had two very good football teams. The Red Lion team played in the field behind the Angel Inn and the Sunday School team played in a field at St Helena, owned by Mrs Oates. They stripped at the Wesleyan chapel in Norfolk Hill and walked up to St Helena in all weathers and played some good games there. Beevers, Baileys, Hubbards, Nightingales, Eyres, Gages and others made up the teams and wonderful sports they were. Johnsons, Sheldons, Marsdens, Hobsons, Platts, Wilsons, Burkinshaws, Housleys and others made up the other team and they often helped each other out. John Hobson had the job of taking them in the wagonette on their away games. Grenoside also had a decent cricket team and played first at St Helena and then at Middleton. Later the village park was the venue.

Arthur Andrews, born 1900

Cricketing Memories

After recovery from my works accident I organised both a cricket and a football team at Greenhead Sunday School. We joined the Sunday School League but didn't do very well. I was opening batsman. We had Harold Bellamy, Goff Bellamy, Percy Bellamy, three Fulleloves and John Senior – he used to run for me. I was the only man in local cricket who had a runner in every match he played! I fielded at second slip. Sam Shaw, probably the only black man in Chapeltown was our umpire.

When we moved onto South Road in High Green I was asked to play for Mortomley St Saviour's team. My brothers Ted and Albert, played too. We were in the Chapeltown and District League run by the Barnes Hall family who were keen cricketers and had a good side at Barnes Hall. We won the Chapeltown League four years running in the late 1920s and we won the Sime League.

I got married in 1934 and went to live in Creswick Lane. I was invited to play with Whitley Hall cricket team. I opened the batting with Ike Baxter and my runner was Hugh Taylor. We won the Thorne Cup in its first year. It was put up by Willie Thorne,

The Dransfield brothers at a Mortomley St Saviour's cricket match. From left to right: Ted, Harold, Albert and Elijah.

Members of Barnes Green Cricket Club in 1910. Barnes Green were always a powerful force in local competitions.

the local dentist. After playing cricket for three or four years I had to give up because of domestic duties. I am now a patron.

Elijah Dransfield, born 1900

Pitch and Toss

There was a tossing ring in the wood quite near the railway line, run by men from the Westwood Rows and a gang from Grenoside. The man whose turn it was to have the bank, i.e., to pay out if he lost, threw two copper halfpennies into the air and if they both finished up heads he won, but the coins had to spin in the air. If at any time the coins were in the air and any man in the betting ring wasn't satisfied with the spin of the coins, he could shout 'void' and that pitch must be thrown again. And as they didn't trust each other, they could insist on the coins being placed on a thin strip of wood and thrown up without being touched by hand. If the coins came down a head and a tail it was a void bet and had to be thrown again. If both coins came down tails the punter won. The men always played on pay day.

We lads, about six of us, would watch out and be paid by the winner a penny each. Once one man didn't pay and laughed at us, so the next time, when there was plenty of money on the bare ground, we shouted

'Police! Police!' and they shot off grabbing what they could – but they just dare not stop, the penalties were too severe. We then gathered a few bob between us.

Colin Sansam, born 1905

Street Games at Lane End

We played on the street at Lane End at skipping, whip and top and marbles. We made skipping ropes with string retrieved from orange boxes – plenty of knots in them! If we had a bit of coloured chalk we drew on our tops and whipped them to show magical patterns. Our marbles were usually brown earthenware ones or much larger white 'potties' and we scooped out holes in the ground for our game of marbles. If anyone had a glass marble, a glass 'alley', it was envied and treasured. When dad obtained some metal hoops and hooks we would gallop up and down for hours.

Mr and Mrs Newton Drew lived in Staindrop Lodge and once a year Mrs Drew sent the Rolls Royce into our yard and it was filled up with as many children as it could hold. Back at the Lodge the lady of the house came out and led us into the orchard where she told us we could have all the apples that had fallen from the trees. We all came out of the orchard with pockets and jerseys bulging with fruit, and we were returned by car. The ride was only short but it was much appreciated. When we were a little older the local farmer Mr Henry Binder, would send a horse and dray to take us to the farm to pick potatoes or to pull up weeds. For our day's work we received 2s 6d

Staindrop Lodge, built in 1806 by George Newton, a founder of Newton Chambers and named after his birthplace in County Durham. It was extensively enlarged and altered in 1904 by Thomas Chambers Newton, his grandson.

Walter Ibbotson and his family outside his general store at the top of Wortley Road, High Green. Besides the shop, he ran a wagonette business transporting people and goods to and from railway stations and other local destinations.

and a turnip. This was appreciated by our mum.

Len Smith, born 1911

Holiday Memories, High Green

For our family holiday we used to go to Cleethorpes – we were there at the outbreak of the First World War! Later holidays were spent at Blackpool. The journeys there and back must have been nightmares for the men who had to carry the luggage to either Westwood or Chapeltown station. I once remember the train being delayed and Ibbotson's wagonette had been to meet the train at Chapeltown but we all missed it so we had to walk with the luggage, plus a steady downpour. I remember this occasion because I was wearing a particularly obnoxious hat and it was ruined. Was I glad!

The highlight of the summer was the 'Club Treat'. The children who were eligible to go were very much envied by the others. There was a visit to High Green cinema and then the children trooped back across the road to High Green Working Men's Club where large bags were handed out through the lower windows. These bags contained a large teacake with a plentiful filling of boiled ham, a bun, a lemon tart and a stick of rock. My gran used to say that many mothers would take the ham out of the teacake and spread it out onto more bread to make a good tea for all the family. Another good day was the Club Sports. There was always a marquee and a band for dancing in the evening. I can also remember a travelling circus passing through High Green and the elephant being fed with buns at the Co-op corner.

Pa used to tell me about the Mummers play which he and his cronies performed round the pubs at Christmas when they were lads. They hadn't any costumes so they used to turn their coats inside out and their caps back to front. It was the play well known in Yorkshire about St George and included a doctor, King Alfred and Giant Sticklebutt. Pa could recite it all the way through for as long as he lived. These were some of the words:

I am the doctor and I cure all ills
Gollop down me potion and chew on me pills
I can cure the palsy, the spleen, and the gout
I can cure you within, I can cure you without.
If there's ought in your belly that's making you ill
I can get to it soon with the help of my drill.
Up, Giant Sticklebutt, up on your feet
Up, good King Alfred who the giant did beat
Get up St George, old England's knight
You have wounded the dragon and finished the fight.
We'll kill you old dragon and poison old Nick
This Yuletide the two of you will be mortal sick.

Young men, old men
We are very cold
Inside and outside
We are very cold
If you don't give us silver
Then give us gold
From the money in your pockets
Young men and old.

Clara Housley (née Marshall), born 1911

Ecclesfield Pastimes

It was safe to play on the street because there was hardly any traffic, and only one bus called Lord Kitchener from Durant's Garage in Chapeltown. I shall never forget when the first gas lamp was erected. It was just across the road from our house, near the trough, which was there for horses to drink

The Picture Palace, Ecclesfield with its neighbouring gas lamp and horse trough.

Ecclesfield Great Central railway station and staff.

from. The trough was in memory of Thomas Jeffcock. We often played under the lamp.

In the middle of our row of houses there was a jennel. If it rained we spent hours there playing 'Hiddy Pot'. The houses were built of stone so there were lots of ledges and hollows to hide a small piece of stone or pot. The person who was 'on' closed their eyes until the piece of pot was hidden. They then had to search for it whilst everyone else would tell them if they were getting colder or warmer. Sometimes it took ages.

A special treat was the Sunday school trip to Cleethorpes on the train. It would be 9d for children and 1s 6d for adults, if you attended regularly. I don't think any of us were able to sleep the night before, we were all too excited. Station Road would be crowded with people. Once the train came there was plenty of shoving and pushing to get a good seat. How we enjoyed it!

My dad was very strict with us. No swearing in the house, no cards or domino playing on Sundays, yet he would go to the Arundel and have to be fetched out for his dinner, sometimes at two o'clock. He did not like that at all. We had to jump up at the window to attract his attention, then get out of the way a bit smart, or we would get a thick lug. Before the pubs reopened on Sunday night, we all had to sing hymns. Mind you we all loved singing, and my parents used to sing in harmony, it was lovely. We each had to take our different parts. If one note was wrong, dad would stop the singing and those who were not good singers had to go out of the room.

Kate Hoyland (née Fisher), born 1910

Sporty Chapeltown

Sport was an important part of life in the 1920s, both playing and watching. There was a cricket club and ground at White Lane, near to where Warren School once stood. There was a cricket ground and a football pitch on Station Road. The football pitch was parallel to Station Road near the Blackburn Brook and the soccer team based there were known as the 'Prims' as they were associated with Station Road Primitive Methodist chapel. They had some good players, the goalkeeper, Bernard Billcliffe, became a professional and played for Chesterfield. The soccer field merged into the cricket pitch which was beautifully kept. Parramore's Foundry had a soccer pitch alongside Smith Street and their cricket team played at the top of Thorpe Hill. Of course the main cricket pitch was the Thorncliffe ground on Loundside. On an afternoon mid-week, when the shopkeepers closed for a half day, a team known as Chapeltown Tradesmen played cricket there. Some well known names taking part were Tom Kay, Harold Kay, Swift Bell, Wilf Cooper, Edwin Bertram and Bill Croft. The Thorncliffe Football ground was at Lane End behind the now-demolished Bridge Inn.

All the schools had sports fields and a local man called Pat Nicholson started a football competition for boys under sixteen. Each team paid a small entrance fee and at the end of the season the winning team got a set of medals – Pat's medals.

There were two bowling greens – one behind the Midland Bank (now HSBC) and the other in front of the Midland Hotel (now called the Carousel). The Miners' Welfare Hall was built on the site of a row of

Chapeltown Central football team, 1929/30. The secretary was Len Hulbert.

cottages called Moulders Row, demolished after being damaged by floods in the 1920s, and it had good snooker and billiards tables. About the same time a pavilion was built behind the Midland Bank and was used for parties and wedding celebrations. It was also used by a tennis club called the 'Rendezvous' which had two tennis courts.

Eddie Ogle, born 1914

Wharncliffe Crags

Our holiday outings were to Wharncliffe Crags, about three miles away. We would go with neighbours' children, up to fifteen of us. We set off in the morning with some jam sandwiches, a bottle of water and some lemon crystals. We had usually eaten the crystals and all the food before we got there. As a child the sight of the Crags was like the eighth wonder of the world! Climbing up the rocks, finding the 'Dragon's Den', we played for hours until hunger drove us home.

Doreen Smith (née Ashton), born 1911

Ecclesfield Sports and Pastimes

The village supported several football teams. Ecclesfield Red Rose has a long history and for several years Ecclesfield United were prominent in the Association League. Some members later played professionally. Two names spring to mind – Harry Johnson and

Ecclesfield Red Rose football team, 1936/37.

Ecclesfield United football team, 1920s.

Tommy Johnson who both played for Sheffield United. Ecclesfield Cricket Club were a pleasure to watch. The bowling greens and tennis courts were laid down in the park when I was very young. The Black Bull had a full-size billiards table and the Reading Room (now demolished) almost opposite had two full-size tables. The Ball Inn had a three-quarter table and I spent many happy hours practising my skills.

There were eleven pubs in Ecclesfield, all supplied by a different brewery. The pubs were divided into different rooms – the best room, the snug and the tap room. Men in their working clothes were expected to use the tap room where the furnishings were plain wooden tables and stools, a bare floor and a cast iron spittoon filled with sawdust. The beer in the tap room was a penny a pint cheaper than in the other rooms. Cards and dominoes were played every night in the tap room. Most pubs had a piano and some landlords employed a professional pianist for Saturday nights when anyone who fancied themselves as a singer could get up and entertain the company with their favourite songs. The Ecclesfield bandmaster, Mr Sayles, of the Selma Mouth Organ Band used to rehearse at the Griffin Inn on Thursday evenings and we used to sit and listen to them if we could rustle up enough money for a glass of beer (under age drinking, I confess).

Joseph Knott, born 1915

Passing the Time

During the summer holidays the weather always seemed to be hot and we only wore a shirt, short trousers and black pumps. We loved to play in the stream which flowed near Colley Road. We stopped the flow of the water which we called the 'blob' and could get about two feet of water before it eventually washed over the top. We bathed in it for weeks even though it was like cocoa in colour with all the mud. There was a tree on the high bank on one side of the blob and a rope was attached to a branch so that you could swing right over the water. Many boys could hold on together, and inevitably the bottom one often slipped off, or was pushed, into the water – all good fun! One winter the Mill Dam, which is at the back of Ecclesfield Working Men's Club, froze over. We put on our clogs and skated on it for a couple of weeks until it thawed.

On winter evenings, for devilment, we played pranks on our neighbours by stuffing newspaper up cast-iron drainpipes and setting it alight. It made an incredible sound which we called the 'bull roar'. Another trick was to thread a large button onto a length of black cotton and pin it on a window frame. We let the button tap on the window causing someone to come out and look what was going on: we were hiding behind a near-by hedge. A favourite prank was to wait until we saw someone going out of their back door to the outdoor toilet. As the doors were adjacent it was easy to tie the door handles together with string and then watch the commotion. Once, our toilet door got tied to the back door with my dad in the toilet. The air was blue until my mum let him out.

Ecclesfield had a good cricket team and two of my favourite players were Sid Gillott, the fast bowler, and Harry Ridge who kept wicket. The one I liked best of all was Ike Baxter who opened the innings with his brother. Sad to say they played for Whitley Lane!

As I got older Saturday nights were dance nights and we went to the Reading Room for a game of snooker first then up to the Gatty Hall for a chance to meet the ladies. When the American soldiers came we never had a look in. We went all over the place dancing – the Newton Hall, Page Hall and Miners' Welfare Halls.

Lewis Burrows, born 1927

Matinée Time

Periodically, there would be concerts at the Miners' Welfare Hall and the Newton Hall at Chapeltown. There was one concert that came to the Welfare Hall once a year that was very popular with children. This was the 'Gloops' concert. Gloops was a strip cartoon cat character in the *Sheffield Star*. He was as large as a child and always walked upright. He could also speak. There was also his human family of characters to give him full support in their funny production. The admission fee to these concerts was threepence or two special coupons cut from two issues of the *Sheffield Star*. As there was little chance of raising the money for a mid-week concert, our only hope was to use the coupons, except we did not take the *Star*. We rectified this by calling on our neighbours who did take it and who did not have young children. There was always a way.

Occasionally, there would be a concert by the Sunshine Girls. The Sunshine Girls were a dancing school made up of local girls, aged from about four to fourteen, based in Chapeltown. My sister Betty was

The Sunshine Girls, whose performances packed the Newton Hall. The dancing troupe was run by Mrs Wastnedge of Station Road, Chapeltown in the 1930s.

a member of it for a while. The Newton Hall would be full on these occasions, with the entrance fee being sixpence for adults and threepence for children.

Eddie Platts, born 1927

Lamp-putter-outer

Every night John Kirkham used to light the gas lamps on Burncross Road from Chapeltown to Bracken Hill and then put them out each morning. Unbeknown to him there were times when Dougie Laycock followed him in the darkness, scrimmed up the lamp-post and put out the light! John Kirkham eventually caught up with Dougie in Thompson's paper shop, grabbed him and said, 'If tha dus it agean and follers me purrin lamps awt I'll gi thee what for…and tha can tell thi father!'

Phil Timmons (née Kirkham), born 1920

Knur and spell players at the Crown Inn.

Knur and Spell at High Green

Before the Second World War, the game of knur and spell was played in a number of places. One favourite spot was known as Ben Waddy's Park, the area now covered by the Angram Bank housing estate. Perhaps the most popular venue was the field at the back of the Crown Inn, especially on Sunday afternoons in the summer after closing time. When a match was going to take place word was passed round the village. The matches were challenge matches between individuals who often owned their own equipment and made their own spells – a stick about four feet long with a three inch oblong of wood, rounded at the ends, attached to the end of it. When the game was ready for the off, the competitor would tap a small catch at the end of the knur, so releasing a spring. The 'potty', roughly an inch in diameter, would be released into the air and was struck with the wooden end of the spell, hopefully towards the end of the field. The potty which went the furthest was the winner. The distance was either paced out or measured with a chain. Bets were taken on who might be the winner but, as betting was illegal in those days, a keen lookout was kept for the local bobby.

Maisie Hawley (née McPhail)

Playing in the Quarry

My childhood was spent at Warren, which at that time was a very close-knit community. I lived at 1 Top Row. This road ran parallel with Warren Lane. Behind our house, which was part of a row of houses, were gardens and at the far end of these was a deep drop into a disused quarry. This was used by people living in the houses to throw rubbish into, such as ashes from the fires, empty tin cans and jars and general garden rubbish. At the far end was a high rock face with ledges jutting out.

In our school holidays, at weekends and after school in the summertime we played at shop in the quarry. One ledge had two smaller, shelf-like pieces above it – this was always the grocery shop. We gathered tins and boxes from the rubbish tip and put them on the shelves, collected bits of broken cups and plates and this became our money. Sweets were stones wrapped in coloured paper and if we were lucky a broken pancheon became banana split toffee (the pot was dark on the outside and creamy colour on the inside and therefore resembled banana split toffee).

We also had a fish and chip shop. This was in a box-like hole cut into the rock face. There we had soil for chips, piled up on one side of the box, and at the side of that we put small and large pieces of flat stone, which we called fish. One of us would bring newspapers from home. Some would be torn into small pieces for chips open, and some larger pieces for wrapped. We also had a tin for the salt and a small bottle from the tip for the vinegar.

When the men in the houses cleared the gardens, throwing away sprout tops and things like that we made a greengrocery shop with them.

Marjorie Copley (née Andrews), born 1928

Chapeltown Picture Palace

On Saturday mornings I sometimes went to Chapeltown Picture Palace to the children's matinee. It wasn't possible to go every week because it cost 6d, and that was the exact amount of pocket money I had each week. We queued up in a corridor at the side of the building. When the doors opened we all rushed to our favourite seats. The programme always consisted of a travelogue, which we all hated, so there was a lot of cat-calling during this; the news; a cowboy film, perhaps the *Lone Ranger*; a comedy such as the Three Stooges or Laurel and Hardy; and an adventure film, perhaps *Robin Hood* or *William Tell*. There was a lot of cheering and shouting during these films and sometimes the manager would stop the film and put on the lights while he came out in front of the

The Picture Palace, Chapeltown. Purpose-built in the Moorish style, in red brick with a white stucco front, it opened on 23 December 1912.

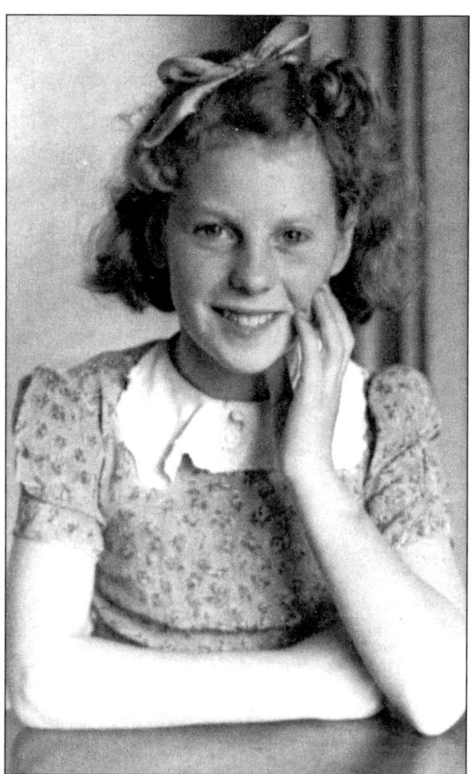

Aileen Bagshaw (later Thompson), aged eleven.

screen to tell us to be quiet and behave ourselves – it worked for about five minutes.

Aileen Thompson (née Bagshaw), born 1933

Making Do At Grenoside

My early years were governed totally by the Second World War. There was a scarcity of toys, sweets, etc. There were no fabricated toys except perhaps lead soldiers. We had to use our imagination or make things and we had a wonderful time. We played together, in substantial groups, in communal games, and games had seasons. In March, for example, it was kite weather. We made our own. Wallpaper was the best material with string and rolled up bits of newspaper for the tail. We made all sizes including a monster kite that flew from the top of Fox Hill to Middlewood Hospital. We could even send messages on them.

We often went to St Helena to watch the men of the village play knur and spell. My uncle, Henry Mollart, was the world champion. Games were also played on the sloping football pitch behind the Angel Inn. This was also where North's feast came after the war. As kids we devised a similar game to knur and spell which was called nipsy. Sometimes we played one to one, at other times we had teams. We also played a team game called 'Tally-ho Dogs', it was a giant version of 'Relievo'. The den was the bottom chip shop yard belonging to Beevers (where you could get a ½d-worth of chips). We set the boundaries: Ecclesfield in one direction, Oughtibridge in another, the top of Greno Woods and Fox Hill. You could walk, run and hide anywhere in that area – the games lasted for days! The objective was to hide and not get caught. If you were caught you were taken back to the den but you could get released by one of your team members if the keeper of the den went missing.

Dave Sheldon, born 1938

The GFS

When I was about nine I joined the Girls Friendly Society, an organisation connected with St John's church. One of the attractions was that we did country dancing, which I loved. It was like a youth club, but just for girls. We went on rambles, played games, had beetle drives, did craftwork, drama and had talks. Once a year there was a great get-together of all the branches in the diocese, usually at York, where we sent in entries to compete against the other branches – handwriting, embroidery, etc. On the day we performed in front of judges at things like verse speaking, and, of course, country dancing. Being a Christian organisation there was no prize for the winners, just a cup which you kept for a year and a certificate. My recollection is that the Chapeltown branch did quite well, though that may be wishful memory.

Aileen Thompson (née Bagshaw), born 1933

Cub Leader, 1945-67

My ambition was to be a Girl Guide – camping and all that! Unfortunately due to the Second World War I didn't get the chance. I joined the Rangers at Ecclesfield when I was fifteen. There were only five of us and we were asked to help with either Brownies, Guides or Cubs – I opted for Cubs. I started early in 1945 with only two cubs, Geoffrey Green and Peter Shaw. I took over the 1st Wentworth (Ecclesfield) Pack and gradually built it up to fifty Cubs and then needed to have two nights per week. Games played included silent tracking, knotting in sixes, Kim's game, observation, treasure hunts, frozen statues, toothbrush and germ. We held special pack meetings on themes such as pirates, South Sea Islands and Robin Hood when Cubs had to invent their own costume and bring or make the appropriate food. At that time the Scout leaders were Mr Harry Frost and Mr Austin, I think. The District Commissioner was Dr Skelton.

My first camp was at Greenmoor when I took about a dozen Cubs and a Girl Guide, Iris Bennett, who eventually became my Assistant Cub Scout Leader. I well remember this camp – did it rain? It poured and we were flooded out and had to ring for Frank Hulley's ice-cream van to take the boys home.

We did many things as a pack. We had pet evenings with a vet, coping with dogs, cats, budgies, mice, hamsters and rabbits all together on one evening! We took part in the district Gang Shows and each year took part in the Winter Rally at the Newton Hall, putting on sketches such as 'Bathing the Baby' and 'The Mariner's Compass'.

When I was appointed District Cub Scout Leader by Peggy Bovill I started 5-a-side football with the Cubs and organised fetes, autumn fayres, day outings and camps. Cub competitions always had themes – Romans, Camelot, Knights – and the winning pack took away the beautiful Wolf's Head Totem Pole for a year. Every year I organised the Christmas party for all the Cubs in the district – 300 of them – in the Izal Factory canteen. We had organised games, tea, film shows and even a balloon man to entertain.

In July 1957 Cubs and Scouts from all the groups in the district attended the Sutton Coldfield Jamboree, a splendid event. 1966 was a special year. On St George's Day Harold West presented me with the Medal of Merit at Hesley Wood County Scout Training Centre. It was also the year we celebrated 50 years of Cubbing and we held 9 events as a district culminating in a special Year 2000 in Chapeltown park. Each pack dressed according to how they thought Cubs would be dressed in the year 2000 and each pack had their own time machine.

Balloons were sent off around the world and the general public came to watch. Packs linked up with an overseas pack and raised money for 12 guide dogs for the blind. Although there was a lot of hard work we all worked together and built up a strong and successful district which I left in 1967 when we moved to Devon. Monica Grinsted was my successor and then another friend Iris Gale.

My husband, Basil Ibbotson, was Senior Scout Leader for Ecclesfield Seniors and they competed each year for the Senior Scout Trophy which they often won. They had special hikes (my husband using his lorry for transporting them into Derbyshire), dinners, camps and visits to Austria.

Elvy Ibbotson (née Layte),born 1928

Grenoside Scouts and Cubs

We met in an old barn opposite the food office. We played 'British Bulldogs', where we charged across the room until we got stopped and 'Blind Pirates'. This was a very skilful game because it tested the hearing ability of one person against the ability of another person to move silently. The 'Blind Pirate' sat, blindfolded, on a trestle at one end of the room protecting his treasure (a metal bucket containing a marble or something that rattled). Another boy had to move from the opposite end of the room and try to pick up the bucket and take it away without being heard. If you were pointed at, you lost. The art of moving silently is difficult to achieve, we tried shoes and socks off, walking on hands and knees and even

Elvy Ibbotson (née Layte) (front), with the 1st Wentworth Cubs (Ecclesfield) at the St George's Day parade and service at Wentworth Church, 1958.

Nancy Bradshaw gives the key to the new Scout HQ on Salt Box Lane, Grenoside, to the Chief Scout, Lord Rowallan, in 1948.

swinging on ropes, we became very ingenious.

Another game was 'Message Carrying'. Boys were sent to various parts of the village and one person was then given a message such as 'The Army is in retreat.' It was passed on from boy to boy and would probably come back as 'Sheffield Wednesday are losing 3-1'! The aim was to make you concentrate. An outdoor favourite was 'Flag Raiding'. Each team had a flag of distinctive colour. One group had the top of the wood and the other the bottom as their position. You had to partially hide the flag, leaving at least six square inches visible. The objective was to steal each others' flag. You could set a defence, but not an obvious defence. Everyone had one life in the form of your neckerchief. If you were attacking and you were seen by someone else and they removed your neckerchief you were out. You had to be very stealthy. Once you had the flag your team had won.

In 1948 the Scouts built their own Scout hut and it was visited by the then

Pauline Cooper, Carol Adams and Pat Cook outside one of the hostels at Bracken Hill Camp.

Chief Scout, Lord Rowallan, to open the new building. I presented him with a penknife and he gave me a penny, which I've still got, an old penny. Nancy Bradshaw gave him the key to open the hut. This building has now been replaced.

Dave Sheldon, born 1938

Leisure time at Bracken Hill

There were lots of children on the camp. My main friends were Pat Cook, who lived next door but one, Janet Jubb and Carol Barnes. One of our favourite pastimes was playing house. We used bricks to outline the room and jam jars and old saucepans to produce slopdosh stew and dandelion clock potatoes. Pebbles became peas or sprouts and grass and leaves became cabbage. We would walk our dolls prams up and down the road for hours.

Carol Limb (née Adams), born 1946

Growing Up in Grenoside

I was nine years old at the time and had just moved into the area from Eckington in Derbyshire with my mum, dad and brother. Young as I was, Grenoside grabbed me as soon as I saw it. It had everything a boy could want – safe streets, loads of fields and woods to explore, a park to hang out in, and a newsagents shop to pick up the daily essentials – comics such as *Roy of the Rovers* and the *Incredible Hulk*, endless bags of Monster Munch crisps and all the sweets you could eat. Eckington was soon forgotten.

We moved into a house on Grenobank Road and as young lads do I quickly set about staking my claim on the place. My brother nicked the bigger bedroom so I made sure the loft in the garage became my personal den.

I soon made friends. A load of boys my age lived in Grenfolds Road, Rojean Road, Middleton Lane, Swift Road and other surrounding streets. My garage loft proved a big hit with these lads too. I'd often be up there with two or three other friends, and more often than not, we'd end up being chased out of there by my mum for making too much noise or getting up to no good.

Another meeting place we had was the 'shale', a small area of rough land off Middleton Lane bordered by garages, houses and a steep bank of grass and nettles. We used to have endless games of football on there which would only be stopped if we had to go in for tea or if it got too dark to play. Scores were normally around 16-14. The 'shale' was our Wembley, Hillsborough and Bramall Lane. We formed a team called Shale Cosmos – named after the great Brazilian side – and we idolised the Wednesday and United players of the era such as Gary Bannister, Terry Curran, Chris Turner, Keith Edwards and Alec Sabella. We also played cricket on there and lost hundreds of balls in the nettles.

The fields between Cinder Hill Lane and Wheel Lane hold some great memories for me. A gang of us used to play a chasing game around there called 'hares and hounds', there was a tree house to climb into, and in winter a steep sloping

Paul Quibell and his 'Chopper' bike.

The 'Lighter Nights' concert group outside Greenhead chapel, Chapeltown, c. 1953.

field made a brilliant sledging run, skid patch, and a venue for some legendary snowball fights.

But with Grenoside being so hilly, cycling was a must. I can remember taking my 'Chopper' bike on high speed 'burns' down Whitley Lane, flying round blind bends with no brakes. Somehow, I never thought cars could be coming up in the other direction. I used to meet my friends on their bikes and together we made the 'little woods' at the top of Cinder Hill Lane a Donnington Park racing circuit with everybody wanting to be a Barry Sheene. Dave, my brother, had a racer, as did a number of other lads. Some kids rode 'Grifters', but back then, 'Choppers' were the coolest thing on two wheels.

Looking back, Grenoside lacked nothing. As children, we could be out late and not worry about anything happening to us. The area was safe and we knew it. And the early '80s, with bands such as Madness, Adam and the Ants and Duran Duran filling the airwaves and *Minder*, *The Dukes of Hazard* and *Starsky and Hutch* on TV every other night, they really were great days.

Paul Quibell, born 1971

CHAPTER 7

Special Times

Chapeltown Silver Prize Band outside Chapeltown Miners' Welfare in their new uniform in the early 1930s.

Ecclesfield Feast Week

Every year in the 1920s in the first week of June a field owned by the Ball Inn was occupied by the fun fair, John North's amusements on tour! This was a very exciting time for us, our only other excitement being the annual day trip to Cleethorpes or Skegness with the Sunday school. We knew when the fair was due and some of us used to rush out of school at four o'clock on the Wednesday and run up to Thorpe Common to meet the first load from Greasbrough. The magnificent steam engine trundled along pulling three or four trailers at a walking pace and we accompanied it to the Ball Inn. One year a rival amusement fair set up on land behind Dam Row and Mill Road. The main ride was mysteriously burned down one night! The

Left: *'The magnificent steam engine trundled along pulling three or four trailers at a walking pace and we accompanied it to the Ball Inn.'* Right: *Eddie Platts in his bandsman's uniform.*

fair used to remain a week. Mr North had two very attractive daughters but they wouldn't have anything to do with us village lads!

Joseph Knott, born 1915

Chapeltown Band

My father played with the Chapeltown Silver Prize Band – as did his father before him – and when I was about eight years old he brought a cornet home for me. As soon as I was able to play it I also joined the band.

My favourite time in the band when I was a youngster was Christmas. We spent Christmas Day, Boxing Day and sometimes New Year's Day going round the Chapeltown area playing carols. There was no television in those days, so people had no difficulty hearing the band playing in the street. They gave as generously as they could afford into our collection boxes and occasionally we would be offered a drop of Christmas cheer. When we played outside the larger houses where the more affluent people lived, we would play their requests and were rewarded with a subscription of five or ten shillings. But the best place of all was Barnes Hall, the residence of Lady Mabel Smith at Bracken Hill. We always got a pound note there and a glass of good wine for each and every one of us including youngsters like me.

Boxing Day was really enjoyable because the band would call at every public house and there were plenty of them. The pubs in those days were not the fancy theme places that they are today and I doubt if any of them served lager; men were beer drinkers. By lunchtime we arrived at Chapeltown Working Men's Club which on Boxing Day was very throng. We were welcomed into the crowded concert room where we played a good number of carols accompanied by their enthusiastic voices. We lunched there from an abundance of roast pork sandwiches made from breadcakes. On all the tables there were giant jars of pickled onions from which we helped ourselves. I was only about nine years old when I started playing round the pubs at Chapeltown and I found it to be quite exciting, especially having been introduced to the new smells of beer, whisky, wine and cigars. A real Christmas blend.

By late afternoon we were playing round the streets but as it was getting dark we would stop under a gas lamp so that we could see our music. Some of the men would be rocking on their heels and staggering a little having imbibed a generous amount of good cheer throughout the day and, perhaps, at this time the carols would not be quite as musical, but it was all very enjoyable.

At the end of my first Boxing Day, I was standing outside the Yorkshire Penny Bank at Chapeltown with my father, waiting for a bus to take us home to High

Chapeltown Working Men's Club where Chapeltown Silver Prize Band played on Boxing Day. The club opened in 1901, and contained conversation, billiards, smoking, and games rooms and baths.

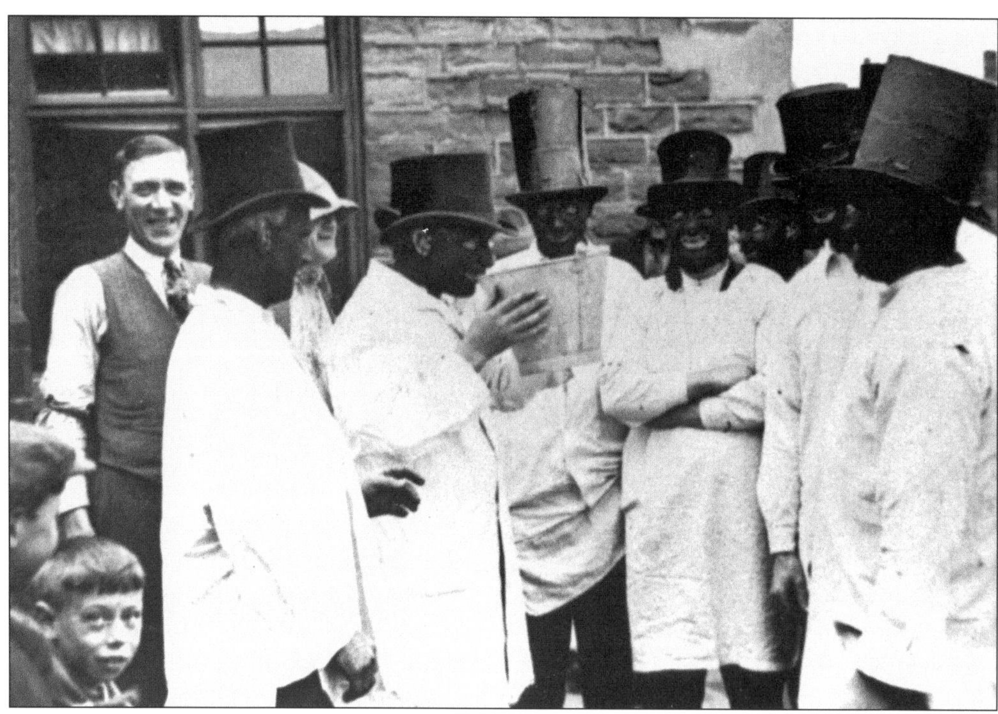

Ecclesfield Plough Bullocks outside the Ball Inn, taking refreshment supplied by landlord Alfred Ridge (left).

Green. He gave me a little packet which he said contained my share of the collection from the previous day. I asked him how much I had got and he told me threepence. This seemed to be confirmed by the fact that I could feel three large coins through the envelope (I am talking about the pre-decimalisation pennies). However, when I got home and opened up the packet, it contained three halfcrowns. I had thought that threepence was a meagre payment but I was quite overwhelmed by the sum of seven shillings and sixpence – today's equivalent of about £25. A few days later, this bought me a new pair of shoes from George Aldham's shop at Mortomley.

Eddie Platts, born 1927

Plough Bullocks

The annual hospital parade was held on one of the Saturdays to correspond with Feast Week. Each street in the village decorated a dray with coloured paper ruffled in a special way. Some ingenious designs were accomplished – a battleship, an aeroplane or steam engine. Prizes were given to the ones judged to be the best. The parade was headed by Ecclesfield Brass Band. Foot characters in costume carried collecting tins and a useful sum of money was collected for Sheffield hospitals. One traditional feature of the parade was the Plough Bullocks. Ten or a dozen men (the bullocks), dressed in long white smocks and with their faces blackened, pulled a plough to which wheels had been fitted. A character would be steering the plough whilst another would walk alongside carrying a stick to which two or three blown-up pigs' bladders were attached. He would occasionally beat the bullocks on the backs with the bladders. He carried a bucket and one of his duties was to call in various pubs and cajole the landlord to fill it with beer. The bullocks would then stop and take turns to drink out of the bucket. Some of them were in a pretty sorry state by the time they reached home.

Joseph Knott, born 1915

Bonfire Night at Burncross

Everyone helped and it took weeks to prepare. We used to trudge up to the woods at Bracken Hill and drag back our finds. Pocket money was saved to buy Jumping Jacks, ½d each, which were bought at Thompson's shop and stored in empty Woodbine boxes. Never forgotten was the time when Harold Goddard tied a Jumping Jack onto the belt at the back of my coat and lit it. I've never got my coat off so quickly before or since!

When the fire had died down, potatoes were roasted in the hot ash. They were usually black and burnt but we didn't care. Eventually, we staggered home cheeks red, eyes smarting and hair reeking of wood smoke. Plenty of time to plan for next year.

Phil Timmons (née Kirkham), born 1920

Barnes Hall Christmas Party

Faint memories of a glittering Christmas party at Barnes Hall still remain and of being taken by my mother although everyone else had a starched nanny in tow. All I can remember (at five or six) is this huge hall towering up to a dome – surely not true – and a staircase sweeping down, a massive Christmas tree and how cross mother was because I disgraced myself. I received the special honour of being offered the beautiful fairy doll from the top of the tree which I firmly refused saying that I wanted a car and caravan instead – a toy I'd been admiring since I arrived. And I enjoyed it for many years, keeping it in pristine condition.

Janet Harrison, born 1932

Ecclesfield Beagles

Although I am now opposed to hunting, as a lad I used to follow the Ecclesfield Beagles and had some thrilling times and experiences. On one occasion the meet was at a private house near Hoober Stand and some of us were transported there by Mr 'Boy' Johnson who owned the timber yard on Ecclesfield Common. His brother Tenor was the chief whipper-in of the hunt. We travelled in the back of his open lorry. After the hunt the hunt members were entertained to tea in the house, whilst we waited outside for the ride home. Being very thirsty I knocked on the back door and when the maid answered I asked for a drink of water which she duly brought. She asked how many of us there were and I told her three. She said, 'Wait there' and after a time reappeared carrying a tray of sandwiches and cakes for us. After a winter's afternoon chasing over ploughed fields you can imagine how that gesture was appreciated by three hungry fourteen year olds – Ellis Jones, Bert Allison and myself.

Joseph Knott, born 1915

Ecclesfield Beagles and followers outside the Ball Inn in 1930. Whipper-in, J. 'Jonty' Sanderson is on the left and chief whipper-in, J.H. 'Tenor' Johnson is in the centre.

Chapeltown Feast in the 1930s

Chapeltown Feast used to be held every summer on the large plot of land behind the Coach and Horses on Station Road and was probably the largest for several miles around. Two of the fair owners' names that readily come to mind, were Marshall's and Tuby's who came year after year.

On entering the fairground there were stalls on either side. One of these sold celluloid dolls dressed in organdie ballerina dresses and on the opposite side there were stalls with things to eat. No visit to the fair would be complete without a bag of brandysnap and those large, sugar-coated jellies with assorted flavours. A further stall would be more likely to be visited on the way out. This was the one that sold small dishes of cockles and whelks and inevitably the wonderful marrowfat peas with mint sauce. The special flavour of these seems to have been unique to the fairgrounds.

Many of the rides were different from those of today's fairs. There were the steamboats (shamrock in some areas), swinging to and fro high above, pausing a little when reaching their highest point, causing the occupants to be hung upside down, clinging onto the rope netting that surrounded the swing boat, in excited terror. The flying chairs, another ride, brought forth loud screams when the engine picked up speed, causing the chairs to be flung out almost horizontally before gradually slowing down again. The cake-walk has long gone, yet it was very popular, mostly with young folk, owing to the difficulty of keeping one's balance. Then there were the carousel horses on which you sat, going up and down, suspended from their twisted brass supports, whilst going round to the accompaniment of the wonderful music from the steam organ with its little figures playing the percussion and beating time to the music. There were also the popular rides which are still going strong today, such as the Noah's Ark and the Dodgems. Most of the rides cost a penny with a bit more for the Dodgems and some of the more daring ones.

Sideshows, which are mainly just a memory now, were always an integral part of the fair. There would be freak shows, including the bearded lady – we had our doubts about her authenticity; the largest rat in the world, which was in fact a coypu, and so on. The wall of death and the ghost train were very popular as was the boxing booth, where the resident boxer would challenge the local chaps for a prize of £5 (much more than a week's wage for most working men). Very few locals came off best.

One year when I was small, I had gone to the fair with my parents, who were attracted to a sideshow where the barker was inviting everyone to go in and see a man who put his head into the mouth of a man-eating lion. I went in with my parents and we were able to

Landlord William Platts outside the Coach & Horses, Chapeltown. Chapeltown Feast was held on the spare land behind the pub beside Blackburn Brook.

get quite near the front, where a large male lion was in his cage. When the show was about to start, a man of African origin started to make his way to the door of the cage, at which point the lion started to roar loudly and my mother made a hasty retreat to the rear of the tent. I stayed near the front with my father.

Before entering the cage, the man knelt down, put his hands together and said a prayer. Naturally, this helped to build up the tension. His next step was to gently open the cage then move stealthily towards the king of beasts, who was watching every movement the man made. At this point the lion crouched down. The African put both hands on the lion's mouth and opened it wide, with the lion's concurrence, obviously. He then put his entire head in its mouth and held it for a few seconds before withdrawing it to the audible sound of relief of the audience. He then exited the cage and everyone applauded. The show was over. I had been totally

Chapeltown Feast at night seen from Chapeltown Park in 1932.

'The African put both hands on the lion's mouth and opened it wide…'

fascinated, yet wondered if it would have been more exciting if the lion had bitten his head off!

Chapeltown Feast was an exceptionally busy time for my father's brother, Granville, who owned the chip shop on Market Street. It was all hands on deck to prepare for the extra demand. There was an outbuilding up the yard behind the house and this was the place where the fish was cut and prepared and the potatoes peeled ready for chipping.

At this stage, we children were able to be of assistance as we had to check every potato and, with a potato knife, remove every eye and blemish before being finally washed and taken across to the shop to be put through the chipper. Rather than regarding it as a chore, we felt important because we were helping out. Anyway, we got our reward during the evening with a big bag of chips and chopped up tripe and cow-heel with salt and vinegar.

Eddie Platts, born 1927

Ecclesfield Hospital Parade

Just after Whitsuntide saw the Hospital Parade. Judging was done on Station Road and my aunt, Laura Stutchbury and Uncle Bill once got the first prizes – my aunt for dressing up as a gypsy and Uncle Bill for dressing up his bike with paper and ribbons. Later on when she was old enough their daughter got dressed up as Robin Hood and won a prize.

Lewis Burrows, born 1927

Ecclesfield Hospital Parade float on Ecclesfield Common, with at least eleven cygnets in the brood!

Laura Stutchbury as a gypsy girl in the Ecclesfield Hospital Parade, 1930.

Whitsuntide in Chapeltown

I was chosen to be Whitsuntide Queen in 1949. On Whit Monday the local churches organised a walk ending in a big get-together in Chapeltown Park for a service and the crowning of the queen. The church whose turn it was to provide the Whitsuntide Queen walked at the head of the procession, preceded by Chapeltown Silver Prize Band playing rousing marches. At various places we were joined by other chapels. We sang hymns, said prayers, and had a sermon, then the crowning ceremony took place. I wore a long white dress which I made myself with the help of the vicar's wife, Joan Gouge. I was very nervous because I had to make a speech and that took the shine off the first part of the day, but once that was over, I relaxed and enjoyed myself.

Aileen Thompson (née Bagshaw), born 1933

Corpus Christi

The Corpus Christi parade was in honour of the feast of Corpus Christi in June. The Blessed Sacrament was carried through High Green. You had a basket of flowers and you strewed them as you walked. Your teacher walked beside you with a big

Crowning of the Sunday School Queen, Aileen Bagshaw (later Thompson), second on the right of Revd Gouge, Whit Monday at Chapeltown Park in 1949.

basket to refill yours. You even did it right down the aisle in church. We practised for hours.

Margaret O'Toole (née Rice), born 1930

Whitsuntide in Ecclesfield

Every Whitsuntide we had new clothes and on the Saturday night my mother would fetch up the tin bath which hung on a nail on the cellar wall to give us children a good scrubbing and hair wash. We had no running hot water, so she had to boil a large iron kettle and pans for our bath, which we had in front of the fire.

On the Sunday evening feeling very posh in our new clothes, we used to gather in the front yard of Rawson's Infant School and wait for Ecclesfield Band to play us down St Mary's Lane and into church. On the following morning, Whit Monday, we would all assemble on Stocks Hill for the sing. We had hymn sheets and the band would be there to play the hymns. My dad used to sing the base very loudly (much to my embarrassment at the time!) After the sing some of us would walk up Priory Road and across the fields to Whitley Hall, where the Grenoside churches would be finishing their sing. After this we would make our way home down Whitley Lane and back up Church Street for dinner.

Later we would all congregate up Priory Road by the Gatty Hall to be met by the band for a long walk round the village. We walked down High Street, Wallet End, Cross Hill, up the Common and into Washington Road, stopping at various places along the way to sing hymns. When this was finished all the children would go back to their various churches for tea and then we would go to play in the park.

Pat Evans (née Hirst), born 1937

Autumn Memories, 1950s

Autumn was a very special time of the year for me for there were so many facets to it. The conker season, where the horse chestnut tree behind St Saviour's church was the focus of many young boys' attention. We threw any convenient missile at those round, green, prickly shells from which emerged those beautifully grained mahogany-coloured conkers with creamy areola. These treasures were taken home, soaked in vinegar, baked in the oven, pierced by a hot skewer and threaded onto a string ready to do battle royal and hopefully to become a champion of High Green School.

Bonfire night also holds many poignant memories. Dark, sticky bonfire toffee and parkin, light brown and oaty, which stuck to the roof of your mouth. We collected wood for the bonfire over many weeks. Everyone brought fireworks to the bonfire and our neighbours would take turns in setting off Rockets, Roman Candles, Jumping Jacks, Catherine Wheels and Flyers, making it a wonderful community occasion.

Gathering sweet chestnuts from the wood near the Five Arches remains with me today, not merely by remembering how prickly they were and how nice they tasted but we had to trample through the leaves which surrounded the trees and I can still smell that sweet, earthy aroma which rose from the carpet of decaying leaves from previous years.

Autumn Fayre at St Saviour's church, Mortomley, c. 1963.

One autumn we were reading a story at school which captured my fertile imagination. It was about Gulliver and his adventures in Lilliput. It was also the time of the St Saviour's Autumn Fayre. Here I could go with my saved-up pocket money and buy the most delicious home-made buns and cakes from the Mothers' Union stall. It was around 1950 and the austerity of rationing after the Second World War was still in operation so sweet things were always my favourite. I could also buy a few Christmas presents, perhaps a peg bag for mum at the handicraft stall. Walking around the thronging hall, for many people attended, I passed the book and magazine stall, and it was here that something caught my eye. There amid the mounds of books and magazines was a book with the title *Lilliput*. I reached over, picked it up, asked how much it was, paid my 'threepence' and eagerly started to open the pages hoping to find more adventures of Gulliver and his travels. I quickly scanned the first page; strange no mention of Gulliver. I turned the next page and looked for him again without success. Try the next page. Oh gosh! Shock! Horror! A lady without any clothes. Is that what they look like? My shock and horror increased when I heard my father's voice say,

Burncross chapel Whitsuntide Sing, 1950.

'What's that you've got, John? Give it to me!' There was no time to give any sort of explanation, punishment was swift. Wallop! A good clip round the lug 'ole and the words, 'Don't let me catch you looking at books like that again!' The injustice! I must say that *Gulliver's Travels* never had the same place in my heart ever again! Worst of all it had cost me threepence!

John Davis, born 1941

Seasonal Excitements

Whitsuntide was always a special event. Weeks before mum would start shopping for dress material and start sewing for Jane and me. Our dresses always had lace edges or smocking. Trips to Sheffield would produce new shoes from Timpsons and a coat from C&A. Burncross Sunday School scholars would sing at Barnes Hall on Whit Sunday and join the other churches and chapels for a sing in Chapeltown Park on Whit Monday. In the afternoon there would be games on the rec followed by tea in the chapel.

Chapeltown Feast was a great attraction in June. Jane and I would queue for rides on the roundabouts, swingboats and helter skelter. We always went home with a doll on a stick, bow and arrow or coconut. As we got older we preferred the Noah's Ark, dodgems and waltzer.

All dressed up and nowhere to go! Clifford Cooper shows off his cowboy outfit and collection of toys, outside his home at Babington, Bracken Hill, in the early 1950s.

In September the crops would be harvested from the fields around my home, the reaper and binder gradually making way for the combine harvester. This heralded the time for harvest festival celebrations at school. All the children would bring a bag or basket of fruit or vegetables to be distributed to the elderly after a thanksgiving service.

As Christmas approached we would make paper chains to decorate the classroom, paper stars to stick on the windows and Christmas tree friezes to stick on the wall. Lastly we would all make a paper hat to wear at the Christmas party. Like most children I could never sleep for excitement on Christmas Eve. My parents would make it worse by telling me that they could hear sleigh bells over Ecclesfield and if I was not asleep soon Santa would not call. Of course, he always did! My presents nearly always included a post office set, cowgirl outfit, sweet shop, a sewing kit of some sort, a John Bull printing outfit, a School Friend annual, a tin of toffees with puppies or kittens on the lid and a selection box.

Carol Limb (née Adams), born 1946

Whitsuntide Clothes

The build-up to the Whit march began about a month before the event when we were taken, usually to Barnsley, usually to the Co-op, always for the divi, to be bought our new clothes and shoes, ready to look smart for the big event.

The clothes in question were always 'a little on the large side' – so that you could grow into them. They consisted of a pair of grey, short trousers (the sort seen on television in those oft repeated post-war films), which came down to the knee in length and were baggy about the beam end. Next came the blazer or jacket. The one which I hated most of all was a brown blazer which was trimmed round the collar and front, the sleeves and pocket with a bright yellow braid. Was I glad when I grew out of it! The worst purchase of all as far as I was concerned was the pair of shoes. I don't know if the shoe making process has undergone a radical change or if today's shoes are more pliable, but the shoes I had bought for me seemed to have been made out of an iron casting from the moulding shop at Newton Chambers. To complete the ensemble would be a new shirt, tie and socks. These items were then stored in the wardrobe and not revealed until the day of the Whit march.

John Davis, born 1941

The Last May Queen

I was the last May Queen at Mortomley RC church in 1964. I think the priest thought it wasn't religious so it just seemed to stop happening. I don't know how I got chosen, I think Miss Smith, the headmistress, and Father Delaney somehow decided. I had to have a special dress made by the dressmaker on Mortomley Lane. It was white, all lace with an underskirt; it had a little mandarin collar and white lace bows all down the front. I wore the same dress for my first communion in July.

I had a cushion bearer (Ruth Barlow) and two train bearers (Leo McHale and Philip Holden). The procession started from church, went up Jeffcock Road to The Circle and then along Greengate Lane and back on Mortomley Lane. The men carried

Janet Maloney (later Brewster), May Queen at St Mary's Roman Catholic church, Mortomley, 1964.

the statue of Mary on a plinth. They all wore their Sunday best suits. I led the procession and my dad walked at the side of me, encouraging me and telling me I was doing really well. It was a big thing, it had gone on for years and people used to come out to watch.

When we got back to church, the statue was put on the steps at the communion rail. I had to climb the steps – I was scared of tripping on my train – and when we sang 'we crown thee with flowers' I had to reach up and crown the statue. I'll always remember that statue of Mary…it was as big as me!

Janet Brewster (née Maloney), born 1956

Grenoside Sword Dancers

Early summer saw some serious preparations in the local schools for the Folk Dance Festival, held annually in Grenoside Park. It must have been 1958 or '59. I don't remember volunteering – you were in! Your partner was chosen for you and instructions issued to report to the hall after school. There were set dances that every school would perform en masse and a display piece for each school – competition was in the air! The day itself was always warm and sunny, or at least that's how I remember it, and full of wonder. There were all the other schools dressed distinctively in their costumes.

There were adult teams from 'foreign parts' with blackened faces, accompanied by strange animals like the 'Tup' and the 'Old Oss'. Sticks clashed, hands clapped, figures were called out briskly and white handkerchiefs rose and fell together. The Morris dancers usually performed on boards set out in a square in the middle of the arena but when I look back on the days, it was the sword dancers who provided me with the greatest excitement. Their iron-clad clogs clattering on the wooden boards heralded the end to conversation. Children and pets were gathered in, ice creams left to drip, the queue for afternoon tea temporarily dispersed. Sensing that all was now as it should be, the captain began his song.

Because we were performers we were seated inside the ropes and close to the boards, so we had a good view. I recall being impressed by the sharpness of the captain's sword and his fox-skin hat and the bright red paisley patterned jackets of the dancers. But the thing that puzzled us the most was how they made their swords stick together when they made the star, and why they pulled their swords from around the captain's neck sending him crashing to the ground. We were always relieved to see him rise to his feet, put on his hat and rejoin the dance. The tramp of the clogs and the lone fiddler was an intoxicating combination and although I was born in the bottom part of the village – on the wrong side of the main road – I was a Grenosider, and this was our very own dance!

When primary school was left behind, summers were never quite the same and it

Grenoside Sword Dancers perform outside the Old Harrow, Grenoside.

wasn't until several years later that I was to recapture the magic of those early days. I had chanced to visit the newsagents one Saturday morning in July and unbeknown to me, it was festival day. The Royal Liberty Morris Dancers from Essex were dancing outside and after lunch I went up into the top village and watched the afternoon displays on Main Street. As I watched the sword dancers, the memories of those far off summer days were revisited and with them the excitement I felt as a boy.

I knew Walter Fleetwood, the team's fiddler and dance master, and declared my interest. My approach was considered and after due passage of time, I was invited to practise. My service with the team hasn't been an unbroken one, but even during my 'sabbatical' years, I never missed Boxing Day to watch the team perform outside the Old Harrow. I recall with great affection, Walter Fleetwood, and his great friend, Fred Myers. Their kindness and wonderful dry sense of humour were a joy in those early days. I must also mention Reg Ward who although he had stopped dancing with the team was to inspire my interest in Cotswold Morris and rapper sword dancing – he being a fine exponent of both.

Although the present team is a little long in the tooth we still have our moments. Six years ago we successfully resurrected the idea of a walking tour of the area. This we do on the first Saturday after New Year's Day and is something we all look forward to – especially the lunchtime stop at Middleton Green Farm. We also have the prospect of new costumes for the Millennium presently being designed by the Fashion Department of Bretton Hall College.

Joe Dunn, born 1948

Grenoside Sword Dancers outside the Old Harrow Inn, Boxing Day, 1998. The Captain wears his traditional fox-skin hat.

T' Big Sing at Grenoside, 1998

Ah din't reckon that Setterda neet i' November 'ud ever cum – ah'd bin 'ummin t' tunes sin' October! But by gum it wor a grand do when it cum! It wer champion! An' it were throng – a cast o' thahsands – well 'undreds – frum all o'er shop, some from as far as America, cum to Grenna ter 'elp keep this ancient tradition gooin. Ah suppooase we owt to gie thanks ter Dr Gatty an' t'other 'eigh churchmen last century fer pushin it aht o' churches into t' chapils, t' pubs, t' streets an' t' ordinary 'ooames.

What 'ud that carol party called t' Big Set that used to tramp rahnd Bradfild, Loxla, Wadsla, Worrall an' Ughtibrig reckon ter t' tapes an' t' CDs an' all rest o' t' electronic paraphernalia? Ah wor readin' 'Ardy's *Under t' Greenwood Tree* t'other day. Fust part's all abaht Chresmas carollers gooin rahnd parish wi' t' orchestra singin traditional carols. 'E wor writin' i' 1870s an' lookin back ter t' 1830s to a deein tradition in 'is part o' country. An' 'ere we are at beginnin o' t' twentifust century an' t'owd tradition's still gooin strong rahnd 'ere. Mooar power to thi elbow Ian Russell!

This is third 'un o' these Big Sings ah've bin ter, an' just like in t' pubs and t' chapils, it fair meks t' 'airs on back of mi neck stand up like chapil hatpegs as sooin as t' singers start singin and t' orchestra starts playin. An' t' enthusiasm o' Ian Russell wi' 'is arms goin twenty to dozen sweeaps iverybody onnards and uppards.

An' what carols! Titles straight aht o' t' Messiah it seeams – *Babylon, Egypt, Mount Moriah*. An' *While Shepherds Watch* ter three diffrent tunes – Liverpooil, Shaw Lane an' Owd Foster. An' owd favrits like *Realms o' Glory, Hail Smilin Morn* an' *Jacob's Well* – but what Jacob's Well got ter do wi' Chresmas ah'll niver know. An' all them bells – singers fro' Thorpe 'ad best on it – the' med a grand job o' *Ring, Ring t' Bells* and *Ring aht ye Bells*. 'Ow ah stopped missen joinin in ah dun't know. An' fowk kallin an' tellin tale an' slakin the' thust i' between singin. 'Ow roof stopped on t' Community Centre beeats me. T' whole thing capped owt, ah'm tellin thi.
Rowl on 2000 an' Millennium Big Sing i' Cutlers' 'All i' Sheffild.

Jon Smeel, born 1938

Ian Russell conducts the orchestra and massed singers at the Big Sing at Grenoside Community Centre, November 1998.